TIME'S UP!
Sermons For Advent, Christmas And Epiphany Cycle A Gospel Texts

BY JOHN B. JAMISON

C.S.S. Publishing Co., Inc.
Lima, Ohio

TIME'S UP!

Copyright © 1992 by
The C.S.S. Publishing Company, Inc.
Lima, Ohio

All rights reserved. No part of this publication may be reproduced, stored in a retrieval system, or transmitted in any form or by any means, electronic, mechanical, photocopying, recording, or otherwise, without the prior permission of the publisher. Inquiries should be addressed to: The C.S.S. Publishing Company, Inc., 628 South Main Street, Lima, Ohio 45804.

Library of Congress Cataloging-in-Publication Data

Jamison, John B., 1952-
   Time's up! : sermons for Advent, Christmas and Epiphany : cycle A first lesson texts / by John B. Jamison.
      p.   cm.
   ISBN 1-55673-423-9
   1. Advent sermons. 2. Christmas Sermons. 3. Epiphany season — Sermons. 4. Bible. N.T. Gospels — Sermons. 5. Sermons, American. I. Title.
BV423454.5.J36   1992
252'.6—dc20   92-6446
                                                                                 CIP

9226 / ISBN 1-55673-423-9   PRINTED IN U.S.A.

**For Pat and Tricia,
I love you both.**

Table Of Contents

Preface 7

Advent 1 9
Time's Up
Matthew 24:36-44 (C)
Matthew 24:37-44 (L, RC)

Advent 2 13
The Man In The River
Matthew 3:1-12

Advent 3 19
Why Do You Ask?
Matthew 11:2-11

Advent 4 23
Mary Christmas
Matthew 1:18-25 (C, L)
Matthew 1:18-24 (RC)

Christmas Eve/Day 29
Your Choice
Luke 2:1-20 (C, L)
Luke 2:1-14 (RC)

Christmas 1 33
Enough
Matthew 2:13-15, 19-23

Christmas 2 37
Watch Your Language
John 1:1-18

Epiphany 41
Just The Facts
Matthew 2:1-12

Epiphany 1 45
Watching The Eyes
Matthew 3:13-17

Epiphany 2 (C, L)   51
Ordinary Time 2 (RC)
   A Second-place Finish
   John 1:29-34 (C, RC)
   John 1:29-41 (L)

Epiphany 3 (C, L)   55
Ordinary Time 3 (RC)
   Question
   Matthew 4:12-23

Epiphany 4 (C, L)   61
Ordinary Time 4 (RC)
   Ka-chang
   Matthew 5:1-12

Epiphany 5 (C, L)   67
Ordinary Time 5 (RC)
   On Being Salty
   Matthew 5:13-16 (C, RC)
   Matthew 5:13-20 (L)

Epiphany 6 (C, L)   71
Ordinary Time 6 (RC)
   For Your Part
   Matthew 5:17-26 (C)
   Matthew 5:20-37 (L)
   Matthew 5:17-37 (RC)

Epiphany 7 (C, L)   77
Ordinary Time 7 (RC)
   Ooo Boy
   Matthew 5:27-37 (C)
   Matthew 5:38-48 (L, RC)

Epiphany 8 (C, L)   83
Ordinary Time 8 (RC)
   Les
   Matthew 5:38-48 (C)
   Matthew 6:24-34 (L, RC)

Transfiguration   89
   Coming Back Down
   Matthew 17:1-9 (C, L)

C — Common
L — Lutheran
RC — Roman Catholic

Preface

One of the guidelines for writing in this series is that you should not use personal illustrations that other preachers could not speak of as their own. I had no idea how difficult this would become. Although writing this collection has been a learning experience for me in many ways, what has struck me the hardest is how closely the "preached" and the "preacher" are connected. On an average Sunday, I am a living part of my sermon. On these pages, I have had to leave room for some other preacher to move in. For the most part I did, but in the few places I did not, please just push me out of the way and preach on.

Don't misunderstand. On Sunday I do not preach John Jamison. The sermon's focus is, and must be, Jesus Christ. However, normally there are more personal stories included so that my folks can walk along side me and give me the chance to point out the Christ I have met, and continue to meet, each and every week. My witness is the only one I feel qualified to preach.

This is not an apology, nor an excuse. It is a plea. Use a pen on this book. Every so often cross out something I say, and write your own preachable paragraph that begins, "There was a time when I . . . ." Lord knows I have worked hard enough to leave the room.

This work was possible because of the unending patience of my wife and daughter, the deeply-caring people of my congregation in Carthage, and the life-changing teachings and friendships of Michael Williams and Jim Fleming. I owe you all much.

Advent 1
Matthew 24:36-44 (C)
Matthew 24:37-44 (L, RC)
Time's Up

Let's start this off with a story. You remember it . . .

If it kept up like this he wasn't going to get anything done all morning. After the telephone calls, that paper-jam in the copier, and now this, he was beginning to feel that it was pointless to try.

She stepped into his office, "Sorry to interrupt you Reverend, I know you are busy, but I need to talk to you!" She went on to tell him about a problem a dear friend of hers was having, and how it would be really "nice" if the pastor could stop by for a visit sometime. Soon. He wanted to say that if people would just stop bothering him long enough to get his work done he would be glad to go out and visit, but he smiled instead and thanked her for stopping. She had gotten his attention. Four other members had stopped by in the last two days worried about the same couple. One of those worriers was even a son of the couple. He believed it was Shem, although he never could tell those three boys apart. And they all said the same thing. They were concerned about them. Well, not both of them exactly, mostly just about the husband.

And that wasn't all. Just yesterday, during his Kiwanis luncheon, the pastor overheard others at the table talking under their breath about how the old man had "gone off the deep end," and that, obviously, "retirement just didn't suit him well." Apparently all that extra time on his hands had gotten to be more than he could handle. Somebody said it looked like "The old guy's oil didn't even register on the stick anymore!" The pastor couldn't help but chuckle along. It was all so strange.

The couple had made great plans for retirement. They would plant a huge garden, he would tend his roses, and they would take plenty of time for travel. But the only traveling he did was back and forth, to and from the lumberyard. In the backyard, the rose bed and the spot staked out for the garden, was covered over by this big, uh, wooden thing.

By the way, the guy down at the lumberyard felt a bit guilty about selling the old man all that lumber. And the nails. Noah was no carpenter, and bent more than he drove in. But the old man had made it clear that if he couldn't buy his materials there, he'd just get them someplace else, and, after all, business IS business.

But none of this was news to the pastor. He had been aware of what was going on for months. It had all started back that week when Noah told his Sunday school class (which he had taught for 27 years) about the dreams he had been having. Since that morning, a couple of class members had made it their mission to keep the pastor informed as to what was being taught. Each week it had become stranger and stranger, and the pastor had begun to wonder how to talk to the old man about retiring (without hurting his feelings) when one Sunday morning after class he walked right into the pastor's office and resigned. It seemed he just didn't have the time to prepare a lesson each week and still get enough work done on the "project." And, he said without a smile, "I'm almost out of time." It sounded a lot like this retirement was really getting him down.

But about this thing in the backyard. At first the neighbors were intrigued. They all thought it was kind of cute to see the old guy out there climbing around with his hammers and saws, although some mornings he started hammering way too early, and some evenings kept sawing way too late. And it was cute how his wife kept yelling at him about how she knew he was going to fall off the ladder and break every bone in his body.

And it was kind of fun to try and guess just what it was that he was hammering and sawing on. First, it was a deck for the yard, then a greenhouse for the roses, then a garage. By now they were betting on a very BIG greenhouse, but thought there really should be more windows. And no one could understand why he built it to look so dog-gone much like a boat, until someone remembered that his hometown had been over on the river and that it must bring back some pleasant memories for him.

But it was getting way too big. The cuteness was beginning to wear as thin as the sunlight that was getting to the neighbor's flowerbed. It seems that a windowless-greenhouse-shaped-like-a-big-boat casts one whale of a shadow. There definitely was a zoning problem. Those same neighbors had a backyard wedding set for next Monday afternoon for their only daughter, and this pile of wood cast its shadow all over those well-made, and highly-paid plans.

But the straw that broke the camel's back was the camels. And the elephants, and the chickens, and the lizards, and the penguins. Enough, after all, was most likely enough. When they asked about him moving the shadow the old man mumbled between nails "There just isn't time," which left them with no choice.

On Friday afternoon, the papers were filed at the courthouse. They would be served first thing Monday morning. The "Big Boat" as it had come to be called, would be dismantled and carried away in time before the big wedding. So would the old man. This later part was the reluctant decision of the old guy's family who felt that some time in a safe, peaceful setting might help him come to terms with the "stresses of retirement." Monday morning would come as quite a surprise. The family called to ask if the pastor would be there as well, to help them help him understand.

Fortunately, or unfortunately, the surprise came one **day** early. It was midway through the second hymn on Sunday morning. "Crazy Old Noah" was sitting in his usual every-Sunday seat, with his family looking rather embarrassed as everyone smiled at them. The pastor closed his hymnbook and started to reach for his sermon notes. But right at the spot where folks usually sang "Amen," God sang instead. It was a bass note. It kind of rumbled around the sanctuary, and down the street outside the church, bouncing off the bank and the furniture store, just thundering its way to wherever thunder goes. And it started to rain. Now, you need to understand that it NEVER rains around here this time of year. But it was raining. Everyone got up and walked to the doors and windows to watch. The pastor saw old Noah just sit there in his seat. The old fool let out a big sigh, looked up at the preacher and said, "Time's up!"

All that the pastor could think as he looked around was that if this rain kept up like this there probably wasn't going to be any wedding tomorrow afternoon.

Now, every time I wade my way into the pulpit, I look around into the faces. One of these days . . .

It may be a crazy, old, bearded man.

It may be a young, baby boomer, career woman.

It may be a middle-aged, slightly paunched, nobody.

But I know it as a certainty. One of these days, right in the middle of my full calendar and my printed order of worship, someone is going to look up at me and sigh, "Time's up!"

Advent 2
Matthew 3:1-12

The Man In The River

One after the other they didn't show up. A whole string of appointments; a morning full of them. They didn't call and cancel, they just didn't show up! Every now and then I would poke my head out of the office door and my secretary would shake her head. Nothing. It was turning into one of those days.

When I get frustrated I eat. I don't recommend it, but I do admit it. So, after the fourth appointment failed to appear, my frustration level peaked. I put on my jacket, headed out the door and made my way the block or so downtown to find myself a little something to munch on.

The sign over the door read, "Asa's Delicatessen: Open 24 Hours." The sign on the door read, "Closed." I pressed my nose against the window, and, sure enough, the place was empty. Not a soul to be seen. I stepped back looking for some explanation and it was then that I noticed that Abram's Sandal Emporium, one door south, was also locked up tight. And on the other side, Jesse's Grain Supply, where they custom-grind 23 different kinds of flour, the grinding wheels were silent.

And the streets. Here it was, mid-morning and the streets were almost bare. This was usually prime time for the marketplace, but this morning most of the booths were empty, and the few in use didn't even draw the browsers. Now my frustrations were overcome by my curiosity. Something must be going on down at the temple.

I made my way around the corner to the temple square and stood looking at the teaching steps. They were always a sight, filled with dozens of rabbis, each seated on a step, surrounded by their attentive disciples. This morning there was only a handful of teachers standing in a little huddle at the foot of the steps. The argument they were lost in seemed to involve someone who wasn't there, and as I walked past them up the steps I heard one of them grumble something about the "river."

As I made my way up the steps, through the tunnel, and into the temple courtyard, I guessed that the high priests were doing some special ritual or sacrifice and everyone had come to take part. But the vast courtyard was empty, except for one or two tables selling pigeons and goats, and a small cluster of colorfully robed priests huddled under the colonnade. They seemed at the end of the same discussion the rabbis were holding on the steps. They all nodded in some unheard agreement, then steamed past me on their way to the steps. One of them shouted to a servant that they were going to the "river." By this time so was I.

On my way out of town I did find one little shop open, so I picked up a bit of something for lunch, and a bit more for the evening, just in case. This might take the rest of the morning, or the rest of the day.

When I got to the Jericho road to begin the 20-mile downhill trek, I found the folks I had been missing all morning. The road was packed. What made it most curious was that those going down the road weren't sure what they were going to see, and those coming back up the road only said things like "Wow!" and "Awesome!" which gave us the impression that whatever we were going to see was certainly going to be worth the journey.

The nearer we got to the river the warmer it became. I took off one of my jackets and wrapped it around my waist, leaving my hands free for my walking stick and my lunch. As we came near the river, the sides of the road were cluttered with wagons and chariots people had hurriedly parked and left, giving the whole thing the image of the suburbs on garage sale Saturday. I made my way through the crowds toward the river. Most folks I didn't know. They were from all over Judea, and from the villages up and down the river valley. I did recognize several from Jerusalem. That's when I saw you. Remember, we kind of waved a little wave and nodded. Then I saw him.

My first thought was that he was a mousy sort of guy. I mean he looked mousy, or really, I guess it was ratty. He looked like a wet rat, standing out in the middle of the creek with his clothes and his hair just hanging off him soaking wet. This is what we have come so far to see? He was busy talking to someone, then shouting to another. He would dip someone into the water and then turn to the next. So, this is it then? You and I stood there next to each other, not really sure what to do next. And then he stopped. He walked out to the middle of the river and turned to face the crowd on our side. Right down in front were those colorful robes I had seen in the temple courtyard. They seemed to have gotten the baptizer's attention. One of the priests stepped foward, like he thought it was his turn, and the river rat let it fly. "You bunch of snakes! Who told you to come down here and run from the wrath of God?" He waited like he really expected a reply.

That one priest had one foot on shore and one in the water and didn't know which one he should stand on. It was an odd sight. Those of us watching started to smile, partly because of the priest's balancing act, but more honestly because it was nice to hear someone finally calling a snake a snake. The priest finally took a step back toward dry ground as the baptizer took a step toward him announcing, "Bear fruit worthy of repentance. Just because you come from good stock don't ever get the idea you are safe. You want in God's kingdom? Produce!"

I'm not sure who was in greater shock, the poor priest in the front row trying like everything to get out of that river, or those of us watching, not believing what we were hearing. I lost him right after the "bear fruit" part. It struck a chord in me. The greatest complaint I had about those guys, and the reason I didn't take part much in church activities . . . did I say "church activities?" I, uh, meant to say "temple activities" . . . the reason I didn't take part in temple activities was that I just couldn't swallow the shallowness of what those guys proclaimed. I believe in God, don't misunderstand, but not the way these guys show God. The way they dress, and act? They seem to think they are God's gift to civilization. They have made our lives miserable often enough. It made us smile to see them brought down a notch.

Then the baptizer took a step back, and turned to the rest of us. By the way, Matthew doesn't tell us about this part. He leaves us smiling. But Luke records more conversation taking place along the creek that morning and it is only fair, I guess, that we remember it, too.

Anyway, he turned to the rest of us. "And for you," he began. Now would be the other side of the coin. It would be something like "Keep up the hard work!" or "It is not so important what you do, as long as you don't hurt anyone." But, instead, it was "And for you. Any of you that has two coats, give one of them to one of those who has no coat." You glanced at the extra coat I had wrapped around my waist and I looked at the one you had folded up under your arm. We stood there surrounded by people who had no coat at all. Surely he isn't serious. This is just an illustration, one of those "Let's pretend" things we use to get a point across. I mean, if we give one coat away what will we wear when we go back up the mountain on the way home tonight? Doesn't he know it gets cold up there? And why was he staring right at us?

I got frustrated. I reached into my bag for something to munch on. "And he who has food, share with him who has no food." My hand froze on the candy bar I had brought for lunch. Now surely you are not referring to us again? What difference is that going to make with all these people. But he was quiet, like he was waiting for me to do something.

At this point we will change back to Matthew's story. He leaves all this part out and lets me smile longer, and since I am the preacher here, I can change gospels like I change channels on television. So, back to Matthew we go.

Besides, the rest is a haze anyway. He went on talking about somebody coming after him, or following him, or something or other, but I guess I quit listening. I edged my way to the rear of the crowd and started walking up the road. I didn't have the nerve to put on the jacket that hung around my waist, somehow it felt too much like a long, purple robe. And I would eat when I reached the privacy of my own house. No, some follower wasn't on my mind during that trip home, and not even now that I remember the story. The only thing on my mind was, and is, "What do I do with that man in the river?"

What do I do with that man in the river?

Advent 3
Matthew 11:2-11

Why Do You Ask?

This passage has puzzled me. The story is pretty simple; John the Baptist sends some of his followers to talk to Jesus, to ask him if he is really the Messiah they have been waiting for, or if they should keep looking. Rather than getting into a bunch of theological jargon, which God's Son could probably do even better than most preachers, Jesus simply tells them to look around at what they see going on and decide for themselves. What they see is amazing; the blind are receiving sight, people who haven't walked in years are playing Ring-Around-the-Rosie, untouchable lepers are hugging and kissing their children, deaf people are standing over there swapping stories, some caskets are lying open over next to a big rock and the contents are up walking around, and the poor are hearing a sermon that makes them smile. It is straight out of the book of Isaiah. This Jesus most definitely is the Messiah! The rest of the passage tells about some comments Jesus made about John, pointing out just how special a role he had played in the unfolding drama. That's the story.

So what is my problem? I have always wondered why John had to send his followers to ask Jesus who he was. Wasn't it only a few months ago that the two of them met by the river and the baptist got all excited and announced, "Look over there! He is the Lamb of God, who takes away the sin of the world." That's the way the gospels record it anyway. Why is it that he has to send these guys now? Wasn't he sure anymore, or what?

Some suggest that this is just one of the mysteries of scripture. They say that perhaps there are two different traditions about how John and Jesus met; one at the river, and one this way. Some suggest that the confusion comes from the fact that each of the four gospel writers tell the story in a slightly different way, and we can't be sure which one is actually the way it happened. One thing we do know. Puzzles like this certainly cause some people to wonder if you can understand or believe any of what this Bible has to say.

I see another possible explanation for John's question. Maybe he forgot. Maybe he did recognize Jesus at his baptism, and now, a few months later, he just forgot. You have to wonder, however, what could make a man forget that Jesus was the Christ. That seems pretty unforgettable. The best way to answer that may be to look at what makes us forget who he is. Maybe that will help.

Shelly was a new Christian. She had just gone through a religious experience that totally changed her life, and as a part of her new life she wanted to become a part of the church. She was running on high speed, and had high hopes. She was going to save the world, or at least the part of it she could reach. She watched her language. She pronounced Jesus with seven syllables, and made sure to use the word "blessed" at least once in every sentence. She started attending Bible studies and promptly made everyone there uncomfortable. But she meant well. No one could blame her for her enthusiasm, because she had just recognized who Jesus was, and we could all remember how that felt. Then Shelly came to a church board meeting.

She bowed her head during the opening prayer, and then studied the minutes of the previous meeting like they were holy scripture. She listened intently to the various committee reports, and nodded as though she understood it all. Then came Phil.

Everyone knew what happened when Phil opened his mouth, you just never knew what the topic would be. Everyone knew except Shelly. Tonight the topic was the new church budget. Phil started out on the money being wasted on those expensive children's bulletins "that don't do anything anyway!" and ended up reminding everyone of how different it was back when Pastor Ludlan was there. Everyone grinned at each other. "There goes Phil again. He'll get tired in a minute and wind down." Everyone but Shelly that is.

She was amazed. This was the "church." The bubble had been burst, and the air fizzled out all over the room. That was the night Shelly began to wonder who Jesus was again. This wasn't what she expected from a Messiah, so maybe she had been mistaken. Maybe Jesus was a "good man," and still worth believing in, but not really a Savior.

But John the Baptist was no newcomer to the movement. And neither was Glen. Glen had been a figurehead in the church and community for 65 years. There were few in town who had not, at some point in their lives, been touched and strengthened by Glen. He was a Christian's Christian, and was admired and praised. His living room wall was covered with plaques and certificates from charitable service organizations, and even one from the governor. Glen seemed to know full well who Jesus was, and sought to serve him. Then he became ill.

Glen was nearly 90 years old and had not been sick more than a few hours of those 90 years. Then the doctor mentioned cancer. At first Glen nodded and said that after 90 good years he had no complaints, but as days passed he grew quiet, the smile left his face, and the love left his eyes. He worried constantly, and complained just a bit more than that. "I've tried to do good," Glen said one morning, "but I just don't see why God would do this to me. This isn't what I expected at all. Maybe I've been wasting my time." After traveling alongside him for nearly 90 years, Glen was now having second thoughts about who this Jesus really was. He expected better treatment from a Messiah.

Most of us do, don't we? We get this comforting idea that if we follow the Messiah life will somehow be smoother, or at least all fit together in some "good" way. Then we run smack into the reality that the only guarantee Jesus made to us had to do with the activities that come after this life. In fact, Jesus very clearly expected that his followers would have a harder time getting through this life than those who walked away. But we still have these expectations of a "Savior" and when Jesus doesn't meet them we begin to wonder if he is really who we thought he was. There are thousands of empty church pews that used to be full of people who believed in Jesus Christ. But then he didn't live up to their expectations and they went home. Their families still fought, they still had some frightening decisions to make, and they still couldn't make ends meet on a budget. They began to wonder if they had made a mistake with Jesus.

Maybe that's what happened to John. He said that he had come to baptize with water, and that the one following him would baptize with "fire from heaven." So where was the fire? So far there wasn't even smoke. So far, the Pharisees and Sadducees were still in charge of the faith, and Rome was still in charge of the government. In fact, instead of bringing in the kingdom, Jesus had kept pretty quiet up north while John got himself arrested and thrown into one of Herod's dungeons on a mountaintop down by the Dead Sea. That might make a person ask some questions. Is this any way for a Messiah to behave?

At least I hope that's what happened with John. If John the Baptist, as high up as he ranked, still had some questions, maybe there is room for me and mine.

Advent 4
Matthew 1:18-25 (C, L)
Matthew 1:18-24 (RC)

Mary Christmas

So, where are the shepherds? And what about the "multitude of the heavenly host" shining their glory on everyone and breaking into song about God, and salvation, and peace?

Sure, there is an angel. One angel, who sounds more like a meditating attorney in a three-piece suit, speaking in one long sentence which tells Joseph he ought to see this thing through and try to work things out with Mary. And that even happens in a dream. But that seems to fit Matthew's purpose. Matthew isn't interested in the trimmings of Christmas. He wanted his Jewish audience to understand that old prophecy was being fulfilled, and had to explain the role of Joseph in this process. All that other stuff might confuse the facts and keep some Jews from seeing the Christ in Christmas.

As for me, I've always preferred Luke's Christmas: the one with shepherds, and singing angels, and swaddling clothes in the manger. We've all become accustomed to that beautiful Christmas on the cards, with Mary and Joseph, dressed in blue and brown, riding the little donkey down the road in the bright starlight to Bethlehem. We smile at the children as they play the parts of the innkeeper and the camels and those other "stars" of Christmas pageants. We light our candles and whisper-sing "Silent Night," and are so moved by the majesty of it we swear we won't wait till next Christmas Eve to come back to church. Now that's Christmas.

But with apologies to Hallmark, Matthew may have it more correct than we would like. For a few minutes I need to remember how it probably really happened. You are welcome to listen in if you would like.

The first thing to keep in mind is that even though it happened nearly 2,000 years ago, some things haven't changed. First century eyebrows raised just as easily as 20th century eyebrows. According to the story told to me, Mary had gone to the well for water. She stood up with the jug, turned around and came face-to-face with a big angel. He had news. It traveled fast. Nazareth was just a small place, perhaps 15 or 20 families living there, and any news traveled quickly. This news would have set a record.

You see, Mary was betrothed. She was kind of married, but not really married. It was kind of an engagement, but more than an engagement. She and Joseph were not living together yet, but if Joseph would have died, Mary would have been considered a widow. It was a firm and honorable commitment. Mary's news would definitely fall somewhere outside the bounds of acceptable for one betrothed. She would be divorced, and could be stoned. Fortunately, the angel had that short visit with Joseph and convinced him to honor the betrothal and trust Mary. That could not have been an easy thing to do, considering all the talk down at the Nazareth Hardees every morning. The decree that came along requiring all Jews to return to their town of birth certainly created some problems for everyone, but at least gave the town something new to talk about and gave Mary and Joseph a change of scenery. Mary Christmas.

By the way, did I mention that these are kids we are talking about here? That's right. Joseph is probably 17 or 18 and Mary is closer to 11 or 12. You need to change the picture of those two riding the donkey. Take some of the maturity out of the face we have painted for her and take some of the hair off of his. At that time, Mary was the right age for betrothal and marriage, but today she would be cramming for a chapter test in her sixth grade Social Studies class.

For reasons we don't need to worry about here, the two of them found themselves on the way from Nazareth to Bethlehem. That's about 80 miles by air, and twice that by road. You begin in the beautiful Jezreel Valley with its fields of grain and springs of water, go through the mountains of the central highlands with their steep and twisting roads and occasional snow, and end up on the border of the wilderness of Judea with its rugged cliffs and waterless climate that absorbs a quart of water from your body each hour simply by your breathing.

Did I mention Samaritans? Contrary to what their son would teach in a few years, Mary and Joseph knew there was no such thing as a "Good Samaritan." The hatred between Samaritan and Jew went back to Babylonian days. Even now, our now, it is often seen that when a Jew happens to walk across the property of a Samaritan, the owner runs out, throws straw on the footprints, and sets fire to it to burn away any trace of the hated contact. For several nights Joseph sought to find a resting place for his young Jewish "bride" in Samaritan land. Mary Christmas.

And take Mary off that donkey. If they were fortunate enough to have one, Joseph would have been riding, and Mary would have been walking along behind. The old culture is amused by our shock, but it is doubtful that we need to worry about it. Donkeys were "rich-folk" transportation, and these were "poor-folk" travelers. Remember later, when Mary and Joseph take their new son to the temple to present the offerings to God, thanking him for the birth? Leviticus states the sacrifice is to be a lamb, one year old. But, if you cannot afford a lamb, then two doves or pigeons will do. Luke reminds us that Mary and Joseph present the "poor" offering of birds in the place of the lamb. There was probably no donkey either.

And don't dress Mary in that pretty blue robe she posed in for the Christmas card photo. The dye for the color blue came from the murex shell found over near Caesarea Maritima. You poked a pin in the top of the snail shell and out dripped a bit of blue coloring used to make the dye. It took 10,000 shells to fill one thimble-full of dye. It was expensive, and reserved for the rich and royal. Put her in shades of tan, nine-months pregnant, on foot, a long way from home. Mary Christmas.

Ah, Bethlehem! At last a warm meal, a warm bath, and a warm bed. But there was no room. And, there was no inn-keeper. The word we have read as "inn" is the same word used later to describe the room Jesus entered to celebrate his last supper. There, it is better translated as "guest chamber." Most homes had a special room that served as the eating and sleeping quarters for guests. Mary and Joseph's family home in Bethlehem apparently had one, too. The family home also apparently had too much family coming back for the census, and there was no room for them in the guest chamber. Fortunately for Mary and Joseph however, many homes around Bethlehem were built up against caves in the hills. The front, man-made part of the house served as the living chambers for the owners, while the cave served as furnace, air conditioner, and a safe place to keep the animals during poor weather. The two sections of the house were separated by a small fence to control where the animals wandered, and against the fence were placed stone mangers so the animals could be fed and watered easily. You can still walk through the small cave that Mary spent the night in. It is a lot prettier now than it was then. The smoke from the oil lamps is gone, and the smell of 2,000 years of incense has finally overcome the smell of sheep and goats and chickens. But that night it was home. A baby was born and placed over in one of those stone mangers to keep the animals from stepping on it. Mary Christmas.

This was probably Mary's Christmas. Knowing these things has begun to change the way I look at Christmas. I'm not trying to destroy those pretty visions that dance around in our heads. I'm not saying you need to go out and buy drab, depressing cards and mail them with drab, depressing little stamps on them. I just want to be like Matthew and cut away some of the tinsel to see what this Christmas thing really means. It wasn't easy then, and still isn't now.

I am not trying to pull the rug out from under your Christmas. I'm trying to remember that Christmas is coming even for those folks who do not have a rug to pull. Mary Christmas!

Christmas Eve/Day
Luke 2:1-20 (C, L)
Luke 2:1-14 (RC)

Your Choice

He stood on the steps and waved. He nodded to those cheering to him from below, and took a deep breath as if to soak up their praise.

And he deserved it. He had taken a good thing and made it better. Much better. He had created an empire like no one had ever seen, or would see again. He had the touch. He always seemed to know exactly the right thing to do and the right time to do it. It was more than shrewdness, it was wisdom. Like that time he traded those 10 old cities up north to King Hiram of Tyre for $3,600,000 and another fortune in cedars of Lebanon, delivered. Hiram had floated those trees all the way down the coast before he visited the cities and saw their real value. By then it was too late. If he only had the wisdom.

The trees were used to build a palace and a great temple, overlaid in fine gold, ivory and precious gems. No silver was used as it was simply too common. It might be fine for the homes of the common folk, but not for the home of the king. And our king built a fleet of ships that sailed to such places as Arabia, Africa and perhaps even India. They returned from one trip carrying $12,600,000 in gold alone. That's in addition to the tons of ivory, sandalwood, all kinds of spices, precious gems and peacocks. Yes, peacocks. They added some color to the place.

One year's income for our ruler amounted to $19,980,000. That, of course, does not include the monies from the traders, the merchants, and the taxes from all the various kings and governors in all the various lands. Our boy also built some 48,000 stalls for his chariot horses and his 12,000 horsemen.

The daily provisions for his household included 185,000 bushels of fine flour, 370 bushels of meal, 10 fat oxen, 20 pasture-fed cattle, 100 sheep, and that does not include various harts, gazelles, roebucks and fatted fowl. That was enough for the king, his wives, all 700 of them, as well as his 300 part-time wives they called concubines.

Stories of this great king traveled as far as his ships, and some found it hard to believe they were true. One who doubted was the queen of a land known as Sheba. To answer her doubts, she paid a visit to this empire, bringing with her a small gift of $3,600,000 in gold, and more gems and spices than ever given before, or since. She was not easily out-glitzed. But after a few days with our king she saw that the stories were more than true, in fact they barely broke the surface. As she prepared to leave, the king's departing gifts to her amounted to everything she had ever wanted, including, we are told, a son by the king which will have to wait for another story. She loaded up her wagons and formed a parade out of the great city of the great king, and historians wrote that as she looked back at his great accomplishments "there was no more spirit within her."

So the great king stood on the steps and waved as she pulled away. He nodded to those cheering below and soaked up their praise. He paused a moment and glanced around at all that surrounded him, then turned, walked up the steps, and entered the great palace. He walked through the great foyer with the gold, ivory and peacocks, and made his way to the library, where he sat down with pen and paper and began to write. He wrote, "Meaningless. It is all meaningless. For all his toil, his toil under the sun, what does a man gain by it? The sun goes up, the sun goes down. The wind blows here, and the wind blows there. Meaningless. Is there nothing new under the sun?"

This is our story. The words could have been written 5,000 years ago, or yesterday. Some are adding chapters here this morning. You see, this is no new battle, and don't misunderstand, it IS a battle. There are two kingdoms around here, and according to the rules you can only belong to one at a time. The greatest choice you make in your life is to which kingdom you will belong.

Both kingdoms have a lot to offer. The one offers fine gold and houses, fast chariots and horsepower, even peacocks and CD players. There is fame, and prestige, and promotion, and power. This is the kingdom of Caesar Augustus. You can stand and make decrees, forcing millions of people to travel millions of miles. There was only one reason a ruler took a census, and that was to find how many young men were available for military service. There was more land yet to conquer, and more was better, and is better in Caesar's kingdom. "So in those days a decree went out from Caesar Augustus that all the world should be enrolled." That's the power the kingdom offers and some of us find it too attractive to pass by.

Some of us know what it feels like to be in over our heads because of wanting more. It is amazing. Years ago we only dreamed of having what we have now, and now that we have it, we dream of more. Somewhere down inside we know that if you keep getting more, one of these days you will have enough and you will be "there," and "there" is a good place to be. It is a restful place. A happy place. The only thing most of us want more than "more" is rest and happiness. So, we do it for our family, or for the good of the company, but we do it just the way it has always been done. And for a moment, once in a while, it looks like it is working. But it's a lie. All this kingdom really offers is the worry that the more we get the more we might lose. That's what the kingdom offers.

The other kingdom pales in comparison. It is the kingdom of shepherds. These are people who take care of someone else's sheep. There is little time for worry about prestige, or power, or promotion. There are lost sheep to find, thirsty sheep to water, and wounded sheep to heal. With no power there is no need for a decree. The folks in this **kingdom** simply serve and care.

To those from the other side, the people in this kingdom appear rather strange. They are called fanatics, or unmotivated. They are certainly missing out on the good things life has to offer. But there are some here this morning from this kingdom. They, alone, really understand the difference between the two. It is really not that difficult to explain the difference, but it is hard for some to believe. I think someone before me has explained this shepherd kingdom far better than I could. They said, "Behold, I bring you good news of great joy that will be to all the people; for to you is born this day in the city of David a Savior, who is Christ the Lord."

One kingdom offers joy, one offers a lie.

One kingdom offers a Savior, one offers stuff.

You take your pick.

Christmas 1
Matthew 2:13-15, 19-23

Enough!

There are many things that could be said about this passage. It is an amazing story. You have heard it before, but for just a few moments I would like for you to remember it with me one more time.

Christmas has come and gone. The baby is born, the angels have sung their songs and have gone back to wherever it is that angels go after a performance, and the shepherds have gone back to sit with their sheep and tell and re-tell the story of their exciting night in Bethlehem. Everything is back to normal. Almost everything. Everything except King Herod. Herod has heard the story of the birth of this new King, and has made it clear that he intends to eliminate this future threat to his throne. So the angel returns in a dream and warns Joseph to take the baby and his mother and run across the border as fast as their feet will carry them. Just how long they stayed in Egypt, and where they lived while they were there we are never told, but finally after Herod dies, the angel hunts them down and tells them that it is safe to return home. However, now that Herod is dead, Bethlehem and Judea are under the control of his son Herod Archelaus, who was as dangerous as his father had been. So, Mary and Joseph decide that the safest thing for them to do is to forget about going back to Bethlehem, and go straight back to Nazareth. They apparently make the trip safe and sound and that brings an end to this little part of the story.

There are many sermons that could be preached on this story. We could talk a while about the power of this God who can show up in the middle of dreams and pull his people out of a really messy situation. We could flavor the sermon up a bit by throwing in some examples of how God has pulled some of us out of tight spots and led us around the danger rather than right through it. Or we could spend some time wondering why sometimes God just lets us stumble along all by ourselves. There is plenty to talk about there.

Or we could preach about how God sometimes uses people from the outside to get done what God wants to get done. According to the old prophecy, the Messiah would come out of Egypt, and would have ended up in Nazareth. Isn't it interesting how old King Herod actually brought that prophecy true through what he did? We could throw in a few more examples of how people who have no intention whatsoever of helping God, who actually do a better job of helping than those of us who make it our profession.

The idea of prophecy itself would make a good sermon here, or maybe we could talk about angels. No, there is no shortage of material. However, what I believe needs to be looked at now is something that the selected passage leaves out, or really, just skips over. If you were reading along with me earlier, you noticed that there are a couple of verses that are left out of the reading. That's probably because there really isn't much holiday spirit in them. They aren't very Christmasy, and they certainly aren't very joyous. But they are real, and with only a few days remaining until the beginning of a new year, perhaps reality is a good place to be. So with apologies to the fine folks who put these lectionary passages together, we are going to hear the story within the story, the one they left out.

All the rest is true. The baby is born and everyone has gone back to whatever they had to do. It just so happened that one of the things Herod felt he had to do was to kill that newborn baby. Politics, you understand. The angel appeared and warned the family to flee, and flee they did. But then, in the part that got left out, Herod flew into a rage. No one raged like Herod could rage. In previous rages he had killed several of his own sons. He was ruthless. The saying was, "It is better to be Herod's pig, than to be Herod's son." Today we would call him psychologically unbalanced but then they just called him "Sir."

It was in this rage that Herod sent an elite group of storm troopers into the little village of Bethlehem with orders to kill every child under the age of two years. And it was done. From house to house, or in the front yard, they were killed. Now scholars point out that, fortunately, Bethlehem was a small village, and we are most likely only talking about 30 or 40 children who were killed. But if you ask any one of those 30 or 40 families I'll bet they thought it was too many.

Yes, we want to celebrate the fact that Mary and Joseph, and their baby, were safe across the border in Egypt. But we must remember the others. We must remember that long afternoon of funerals back in Bethlehem. We have to remember both sides.

That's the way it happens. We see it every day. You work and work to do something good, something that will help someone, and it does. Then, later, you find out that what you did to help one, ended up hurting another. The angel's warning saved the three, but sealed the fate of the 30. You make the decision to improve your career, which you hope will help your family, but the more time you spend on the career the less you have for the family, and it suffers. You see one of your children needing attention. You make the effort to spend more time with your child, only then to find that another child, or your spouse, feels cheated. Your intentions are the best, but the result is split. It is good here, but not good there. It gets to the point where you are afraid to decide anything.

We make decisions that are good for business, or good for the people, only to find that they are not good for the environment. More animals are nearing extinction, the holes in the ozone are getting bigger, and the water table continues to fall. Boy, this is depressing. It's almost enough to make you believe in evil, isn't it?

And it is depressing. So depressing that some of us have thrown our hands up in surrender and quit. Some have decided that they simply can't decide anymore. Life is nothing more than getting up in the morning and taking your chances. No matter what you do, you lose, so why try? Evil has won. As you might guess, this group is a lot of fun at parties. This group is also missing out on a lot of good out there. This isn't the answer.

Some do not get depressed. They get even. There are some here who have decided that good and bad aren't worth worrying about anymore. "Take care of yourself" is their motto. They go for the gusto, and reach for the mountains, and plan on only going around once, so they go with a vengeance. This group also has a unique ability to redefine good and bad. They begin to understand that "good" and "bad" don't really exist. Anything can be good, and anything can be bad. It all just depends. I'm not sure they could sell this theory to those parents back in Bethlehem. No, this isn't the answer either.

So, what then? How do we continue, knowing that the good will always be shadowed by the bad? What do we do?

We lose sleep. We lie awake at night and wonder if we have really made the right choices. We sit by the bed of our children as they sleep and pray that we are doing a good job with them. We dance and rejoice with the three that got out of danger in the nick of time, and we stand and cry with the 30 who never had a chance. In plain words, we care.

Loving people and caring for them, isn't enough to change the way the world works overnight. It isn't enough to spare the life of the dying, or to bring back the one who has died. It isn't enough to protect your child from the hurts and pains that are waiting for her out there. Our caring isn't enough to guarantee the safety of all the whales in the ocean, or the purity of the water in the ground. Our caring isn't enough to change all "bad" into "good."

But it is all we are asked to do. And it is enough.

Christmas 2
John 1:1-18

Watch Your Language

Everyone liked Linda. There was no reason not to like her. She did everything she could to be liked and it worked. Everyone liked Linda.

It had all started with her uncle, about 30 years ago. Linda was just old enough to understand what he was saying the day he picked her up and said, "You are about the most worthless thing in the world." She remembered everyone in the room laughed, including her mother. The uncle went on to say that she was not only worthless, but ugly, dumb and hopeless. It was that last "hopeless" that hit the hardest. Linda thought that people could get over being worthless and dumb, and in time, even do something about being ugly. But for her it was now hopeless.

The older Linda grew, the more she began to worry about the things her uncle had said, and the more she worried, the less she paid attention to what was going on around her. Since she was afraid of being dumb, going to school was terrifying, and her grades showed that her mind was on something other than her work. A third-grade teacher, probably meaning well, wrote on the back of Linda's report card, "Linda is a sweet girl, and tries hard to please, but just doesn't seem to have what it takes to keep up." Linda read it and believed it. Linda's mother read it and simply shook her head. Linda saw that, too.

Linda didn't try to make friends because she knew no one wanted to be friends with an ugly, hopeless girl. The more she stayed apart from the other kids, the more they let her. Linda's only bright spot was when she could stay after school and help one of the older teachers clean her room. She also began to visit an older neighbor lady, to cook and clean house for her. In fact, Linda ended up with about 15 old people she took care of every day. She wasn't paid, and didn't want to be paid, (or maybe it was that she didn't think she deserved to be paid) and she even spent her small allowance money on things they needed. She helped out a lot.

Every month or so she would also jump out in front of a car, or take a few of the old people's pills. The doctors said that she had some psychological and chemical imbalance that sent her into these self-destructive actions. Inside, Linda knew there was no imbalance. She knew that no matter how busy she was, her uncle was right. She was hopeless. It was too much to live with.

By the time Linda was 30, she had an apartment in a high-rise downtown. However, she was rarely in that apartment as she was always helping out in someone else's. She now had about 20 old persons that she cared for in the building. She gave them their medicine, cleaned their floors, cooked their meals, rubbed their sore feet, and ran to the store for them. They kept her busy, and talked to her. And, once a month when she would hear her uncle's voice again and try to kill herself, one of the old ladies would take Linda into her home and hold her, and care for her, and pray with her. The woman would shake her head and say how much she liked to take care of her "sick little girl." Linda heard that, too.

Linda's friend would take her to the doctors, who tried various drugs, psychotherapy, and electro-shock therapy. But Linda heard them all talking about how they really didn't think there was much hope, it was too "deep-seated," and that she probably didn't have the ego-strength to overcome it. Linda's minister would stop by for a visit and hold her hand and pray that she would have the "strength to endure," and that she would be thankful for the great number of people she had that were caring for her. She heard all their words, and believed them. So she stayed sick just like they told her to.

Isn't it something what words can do? They seem to take on a life of their own. Some words, once spoken, seem to come to life and follow us around wherever we go. Some of us here, every once in a while, find ourselves hearing again a word that was spoken to us years ago, as loudly and clearly as it was first spoken. Some of those words help, and some of those words do not. You look in the mirror and what do you hear? Do you hear words like "cute," and "adorable," or do you hear Linda's words? How about when you knock over a cup of coffee? Do you hear, "Oops, somebody had an accident?" or is it more like, "Oh for crying out loud, you are the clumsiest child ever born. What am I going to do with you?" These are words that come to life and become living and breathing flesh that follows you around.

And words don't just follow children here. Your words come to life for adults, too. The health of a marriage depends a lot on the words spoken by wife and husband. The health of a career is influenced by the words used by bosses and co-workers. Even the health of your body depends in part to the words it hears. The old experiment has been proven over and over again. Take a perfectly healthy person, have a number of people tell them that they sure don't look like they feel very well, and before long you will send them to bed with some unforeseen illness. It works! As a matter of fact, some of you look rather pale here this morning. Just kidding.

What about the words you speak to yourself? Many of the strengths you display come from those little pep talks you give yourself now and then, and many of your limitations come from those "I can't" comments you mumble inside every so often. Words come to life. Words pick us up and knock us down. They make us strong and make us sick.

Isn't it interesting that God knew that? Of all the creative methods God could have used to make creation healthy again, he chose words. "And the Word became flesh, and lived among us." God spoke, and the Word that he spoke came to life. It took on flesh, lived and breathed, and still follows us around, every once in a while whispering in our ears when we need to hear it. God had something to say, and said it. God said, "You are worth it. You are not hopeless. I love you." And that has made all the difference in the world.

How about Linda? Not long ago a new minister came to visit with her. But rather than hold her hand and mourn with her, the new preacher said, "What do you think we ought to do?" Linda didn't know how to respond. No one had ever asked her opinion before. The opinion of a worthless, ugly, hopeless woman doesn't carry much weight. But now someone gave it weight. That simple question, "What do you think?" created a spark inside Linda that began to grow. Maybe her uncle's words had been wrong.

Today, Linda lives in her own apartment. She still helps several older residents with their medicines and meals, but now she does it because she wants to, not because she has to. She hasn't jumped in front of a car for two years. And, there is even talk of Linda getting married to this real nice guy she started dating last spring.

"And the Word became flesh, and lived among us."

Hey! Watch your language.

**Epiphany
Matthew 2:1-12**

Just The Facts

There is a beautiful old tradition about the star in the East. The story says that when the star had finished its task of directing the wise men to the baby, it fell from the sky and dropped down into the city well of Bethlehem. According to some legend, that star is there to this day, and can sometimes still be seen by those whose hearts are pure and clean. It's a pretty story. It kind of makes you feel warm inside.

There are other legends about this story of the wise men from the east. For instance, how many wise men were there? In the old days in the east, they believed that there were 12 men who made the journey, but now most everyone agrees there were three. One old legend even tells us the names of the three. Melchior was the oldest of the group, with a full beard. He gave the baby the gift of gold. Balthasar also had a beard, but was not as old as Melchior. He presented the gift of myrrh. The youngest of the three was Casper, who had no beard yet, but did present the gift of frankincense to the baby. Yet another legend goes on to tell us that after seeing the baby, the three continued traveling as far as Spain, telling the world the good news about what they had seen. These stories bring the wise men a little more to life, and add some color to the meaning of Christmas. They can also get in the way.

The problem with legends is that sometimes they add color to stories that don't need any additional color. In fact, sometimes legends are so colorful, they are unbelievable, and can end up making the entire story unbelievable as well. Kind of like that star falling in the well. It makes you warm inside. It also makes you wonder.

I am not out to ban legends, but I do think it might be worthwhile to hear the story one more time, the way it was told the first time. I need to hear it anyway, and you are welcome to listen along if you like.

It all started sometime after Jesus was born. It might have been a few weeks, or even a few years. You remember that when Herod tried to kill the baby, later he murdered every child under the age of two years. Apparently, he wasn't sure how long it had been either.

One thing we do know about the time is that it was explosive. Every nation in that part of the world was on edge. In historical writings from all over the Orient, we read that nations shared the belief that it was fated that a tremendous new king was about to arrive, one that would rule the entire world. From throughout the Roman Empire, into Armenia, as far away as Persia, the people waited for the king's arrival.

It is in Persia that we find our story. Some years back there had been an attempted overthrow of the Persian government by a group of Medes, but the attempt failed. Since they could not destroy the Persians, the Medes joined them. They were a highly-educated group and were deeply respected for their understanding of science, religion and astronomy. They were good, holy men, and were given the name magi. They believed that the stars controlled what happened on earth, and that if a new king was to be born the heavens would give a sign. Apparently they did.

Just what it was that those early astronomers saw we don't know. There was a brilliant appearance of Halley's comet in the year 10 B.C., and some believe that may have been the sign. There were two tremendously bright times, in 7 B.C. and 3 B.C., when Saturn, Jupiter and Venus appeared next to each other as one star. Such an occurrence was always believed to be the sign of a king's birth, and some believe that is what the magi saw. Others believe that the star was a one-time appearance of something supernatural. We don't know. All the Bible says is "We saw his star . . . and have come."

How many have come? Were there 12, or three, or what? We don't know that either. Scripture never says there were three wise men. They gave three gifts, and from that we have supposed there were three gift-givers. And I'm not sure where we got the notion that they were kings. It must have come from that hymn.

Word of their arrival from the east made quite an impression around Bethlehem. The greatest impression was made upon Herod. He was so impressed that he threw an open house for them as a "Welcome to Judea" party. During the celebration he pulled them aside and confided in them. He told them that he was even more excited than they were about this new king being born, and that he would certainly appreciate it if, when they found where the new king was, they would send him word so he could come and visit, or at least send the family some gifts for the baby shower.

Herod was an interesting character. He was what we call a complicated individual. He could be compassionate. Back during the famine of 25 B.C., he had his own solid gold dinner plate melted down and the money given to the poor. More than once he refunded taxes to those who were having a hard time getting by. But he also murdered his wife, his mother-in-law, and at least three of his own sons. Later in life, when he knew he was about to die, he ordered the arrest of 100 of the most respected residents of Jerusalem, and had them imprisoned with the strict order that at the moment of his death all 100 of the prisoners would be killed. He wanted to be sure people would cry at his funeral.

Herod had the potential for good, but was driven by a nightmarish jealousy. If he saw any threat, real or imagined, he did whatever necessary to destroy it. Now, of course, the baby king was a real threat. These wise foreigners would unwittingly help him carry out the necessary destruction. I have always wondered if those wise men really bought his story. Herod was good, but was he that good? We have all been on the receiving end of one of these stories one time or another, and know that some are convincing, and some are not. But knowing Herod, even if they doubted what he said it probably wouldn't have been too smart to say so. Just to be sure they caught on, God filled them in during a dream and they never sent the message to King Herod.

They did find the baby, and they bowed down and worshiped him. They gave him gifts. They gave him gold, the appropriate gift to give a king. They gave him frankincense, a powerful smelling incense which was the usual gift given to a priest. They also gave him myrrh. This one may have raised Mary's eyebrows a bit. It was embalming fluid. Myrrh was the spice used to rub the body in final preparation for burial. And then they went home.

We really don't know when they came and went. We honestly don't know how many there were, but we do know they probably weren't kings. The star in the heaven may have been a "natural" astronomical phenomenon that had occurred before and has since, and probably isn't sitting in the bottom of the Bethlehem well. Sometimes it helps to peel away all this legend and look at what is left.

We do know that the entire known world was holding its breath waiting for a new king of the world to be born. We do know that a team of the greatest scholars alive believed that the baby born in the Bethlehem manger was that king of the world. We do know that the famous Herod the Great also believed that Mary's boy was that new king. The bare facts were enough for all of them to believe that Jesus was the Christ.

I pray they are enough for us.

Epiphany 1
Matthew 3:13-17

Watching The Eyes

The way it happened in my mind is that he walked into this little restaurant in downtown Jericho, took a deep breath and hollered, "Repent!" Folks stopped eating mid-bite. It got so quiet you could hear the motor running in that tall machine over in the corner that kept slices of pie turning around behind the glass all day. Every eye in the place was on him, and that was what he was waiting for. He started talking, and shouting, and waving his arms, and every time someone would try to laugh at him and go back to their coconut cream pie, he would walk right over and slam a fist on their table, or just stand and stare at the pie eater until their appetite simply disappeared. All this without missing a beat of his sermon.

And what a sermon it was. He started out, "Some of you folks are from around here, aren't you? Born and raised right here? Well, that don't count for one blasted thing in God's book. Your ancestral tree might take you all the way back to Abraham himself, but as far as God is concerned, that won't pay for that cup of coffee you got sitting in front of you." He went on for quite some time, made his way from one table to the next, even the big round one in the back where the Pharisees sat at their weekly noon-time alliance meeting. People couldn't help but smile when he walked around that big round table and called them all a bunch of hissing old women who couldn't spell salvation if they had a dictionary in their hands.

Then he was done. He walked out of the door just as he had come in. Except on the way out he was not alone. Several from the restaurant walked out with him, and followed him straight to the river. From there on it was history. More and more people came, and more and more went back home to tell their friends they had better go, too. By the time they got there, the crowds were huge.

At one point in his baptizing, John looked up to see who was next in line, and when he did he froze in his tracks. There standing before him was Jesus. He recognized him immediately. This is where the story gets a bit hard for me to follow. Jesus steps up to be baptized like everyone else, but John shakes his head and says, "How can I baptize you? You ought to be baptizing me." They debate that fact for a bit and John finally gives in and baptizes him. Then, as Jesus gets out of the water, the sky opens up just like it had French doors, and this dove flies down and lands on him. Then, to confuse me even more, a voice comes out of that same door and says, "This is my Son, who I love; with him I am well pleased." And the story is over.

I have studied this story since seminary days, trying to understand all that it means. What about Jesus getting baptized? If baptism is for forgiveness of sins what does Jesus need it for? Some say he did it as a symbol that his ministry was about to begin. Others say he did it to show that he was just like the rest of us human folks. Still others say he did it to make his mother happy. I understand that last one best of all, but I'm still not sure that explains it. And what about the heavens, and that bird, and the voice? The words are straight from Psalm 2 and Isaiah 42, but I'm still not sure what to do with them. Did everyone hear them, or just some, or just Jesus? This story is still a puzzle for me. I'll have to leave it for the theologians. But that's all right, because when I read it I never get all the way to the end, anyway. My mind starts to wander back there when John first looks up and recognizes who Jesus was. That part I understand, and it haunts me.

It haunts me every time I perform a baptism. When I take a child from its mother's arms and say the words of baptism, I find myself looking into the child's eyes. "Who are you?" I find myself asking. I really wonder who this is that has come to be baptized by my hands. I want to recognize him, and am never quite sure I will.

Is this child a president, or maybe a doctor or teacher? Is this child a mother, or a father, or maybe even a great-grandfather? Is this child a criminal, or could it be the Christ? You never really know. When God claims one of these, you never really know who it will become. All that I know is that one of these days, this little squirming bundle of life is going to "Be." But who?

It's no different baptizing older people. I already knew who they were. I have baptized teachers, doctors, lawyers, truck drivers, disc jockeys and horse jockeys. But as I say the words of baptism I still look into their eyes. I am still not too sure just who they will become. Could they be a healer? Could they be one who will sit beside the bed of a dying old man in the nursing home and continue to give hope? Could they be the Christ? I really do want to recognize him when he comes. And he will come.

And you know, it has gone beyond baptism now. I find myself looking into eyes in some of the strangest places. The old man walking in the snow in his short-sleeved shirt, on his way from Pennsylvania to Nebraska, looking for a job. I am in the middle of a busy day, and don't have much time for old coatless men, but then it hits me. So, I find him a coat, and a hot dinner, and a room for the night out of the cold. And the whole time I look into his eyes. "Who are you, really?" Are you an old man looking for a job, or a con man, looking for a sucker? Are you running to, or from, something? Or, are you the Christ? I really do want to recognize him.

And the 16-year-old girl sitting in my living room on Sunday night. There have been worship services, classes to teach, a potluck meal, three visits, and two youth meetings. I am tired, but there she sits. She has had another fight with her parents and has run away. "But I'm okay" she says through tears, "I can take care of myself." Teenagers! I want to tell her to go home, or at least somewhere other than my living room. But then it hits me. And as we sit and talk for three hours, and finally climb into my car for the trip back home, and then sit and talk for another two hours, I look into her eyes. "Who are you?" Are you some spoiled rich girl who is just pulling our chain, or are you a lonely child, wondering if anyone really cares? Are you a blossoming juvenile delinquent taking us all for a ride? Or, could you be the Christ? I really do want to recognize him when he comes.

Or the old woman who always complains. If I don't go see her enough she calls to tell me I don't care for my people. If I make it a point to stop by to visit more often she tells me she needs her rest and doesn't like to be bothered so much. When we do visit, she tells me what everyone is doing wrong, and how many new diseases she has developed since our last visit. I sit and think of being somewhere else. On my way to visit her I think of excuses not to, and even find myself driving around the block a few times. Then it hits me. As I sit there listening to the complaints and the grumbles, I look into her eyes. "Who are you, really?" Are you a sour old woman who enjoys spreading that sourness around, or are you a lonely child who hurts so much inside you can hardly stand it? Could you be the Christ? I really do want to recognize him when he comes. And he will come!

And you. I even find it here. I stand in the pulpit and look at your faces. Some of you look bored to tears. Have you gotten your afternoon planned yet? Others look as though you are desperate to hear something this morning that can carry you through the week. When we are here together I find myself wanting to look you right in the eyes. I hope it doesn't make you uncomfortable. But I wonder, "Who are you, really?" Are you an accountant, or a farmer, or a banker? Or are you the one caring for the dying mother or the lonely father? Are you a "baby-boomer," or are you the one who slips the envelope with money in it under the doors every Christmas? Are you the Christ?

I know he is coming back, and I really want to recognize him when he does. You know, that's what yells at me out of this scripture this morning, John recognized him! I don't always understand what happens after Christ arrives, but I want to be sure to recognize him when he does. I would hate to miss it.

I'm going to keep looking.

Epiphany 2 (C, L)
Ordinary Time 2 (RC)
John 1:29-34 (C, RC)
John 1:29-41 (L)

A Second-place Finish

When his parents died he was still too young to be on his own. Zechariah and Elizabeth had been very old when John was born, so it was no surprise that it happened, but apparently nothing had been done to prepare for it just the same. The rest of the family had gone north to Nazareth because of political problems, and John was alone. According to tradition, he was taken in by a group of old men who lived in a little village down by the Dead Sea. The place was called Qumran, and the men were known as the Essenes.

No one agrees just where the Essenes came from originally, but most agree that they had come to Qumran to get away from the "corruption" they believed was taking place in the temple in Jerusalem. You could say they were religious fanatics, who spent the days and nights copying scripture and writing scrolls about how one day God was going to send his Messiah and flush that filth right out of Jerusalem. Since many of them were unmarried, it was common for them to "adopt" homeless children, and raise and teach them to continue the Essene lifestyle. One of those homeless children may well have been the young boy John. Years later, when he appears just a few miles north of Qumran, he preaches, "Repent, for the kingdom of God is at hand!" These are Essene words, pure and simple.

And John preaches them well. People travel from all over Judea, even from Jerusalem itself, to hear his message. Not only do people end up getting baptized by him, but many of them stay around and sign up to become his disciples. Some even begin to talk about him as the long-awaited Messiah. What a distance he has come from being the orphan boy from the Judean hills.

His mission was succeeding. People were hearing his words and changing their lives. There seemed to be no end to those ready to come under his leadership. Then, one day as he was baptizing, he looked up and saw that one of those in line was Jesus. The One. The Chosen One. The Messiah. John's replacement. Number one to John's number two. I wonder if he was tempted?

I really wonder if the thought went through John's mind to just keep his head down, keep sending the line through, and not let on that he recognized him? Maybe if nothing was said, John could continue his work. After all, it was obviously successful. He apparently had what it took to do this, so why should he step back and let someone else take over. I wonder if it went through John's mind like I'll bet it would have gone through mine?

Before you get all upset that I would suggest that John the Baptist would do such a thing, just let me remind you how hard it is to settle for number two. Elmer Bernstein was once asked what instrument in the orchestra was the most difficult to play, and he answered, "Second fiddle." You know very well that it's true.

Parents struggle with it every day. Sometimes it is almost overwhelming to accept the fact that the kids come first. Sure, they are dependent upon us for food, clothing and safety. Sure, we sometimes have to sacrifice what we want to see that the kids get a good education, and the extras like basketball, swim team, violin or piano lessons, and scouting. But, what about us? There are days I just want to tuck my head down real low, and pretend I don't recognize that this is my child, and maybe I can just do what I want today. If I look the other way, maybe I can stay number one a bit longer. You know it's true. We have all seen parents do just that. It doesn't work though, does it?

And in marriage. In the beginning we made that promise to make the other person most important in our lives, but aren't there days when you just kind of want to duck your head when those vows come walking through your mind? I mean, sure, I promised to make her needs and wants at least equal to my own, and, sure, I know what those needs and wants are, and could meet them if I wanted to. But what about me? I've had a hard week, too. In fact, in my opinion, my week was a bit harder than hers, and that ought to put me in position number one and her in number two. You know it happens. We have all seen marriages that continually arm wrestle over first and second position. It doesn't work either, does it?

It happens at work, it happens with the neighbors, and it happens right here. Right here in God's own living room. There was a point in our lives when we realized just who God really was. We realized how we stacked up against God, and there wasn't much comparison. We call that one of those "Aha" experiences. We promised to be a good and loyal follower, to pray every day, quit seven or eight nasty habits, and read the Bible from cover to cover. And we tried. We really tried. But somewhere along the way we began to wonder, "But, what about me?"

"What about me?" has become the national anthem of society. Whether it is raising children, raising a marriage, making a living or making a commitment to God, one after the other cries out, "But, what about me?" Position number two has become exceedingly unpopular. Spot number one is the place to be and my rights are the ones to ensure. No, if it were me in John's wet shoes that day when Jesus walked up expecting me to humbly step aside and introduce him as the new "man from God," my lips might have hesitated. So how did John make it look so easy?

John new something that I sometimes forget. He knew why he was there. Everything that had happened to him, from the old parents, to the old Essenes, to the crowds getting their shoes wet in the Jordan, he knew why it had happened. He said, "but the reason I came baptizing with water was that he might be revealed to Israel." He knew why he was here and that made all the difference.

Sometimes I forget why I am here. Sometimes I forget and get the ridiculous notion that the reason God gave me a child was to make me happy and meet my needs. Sometimes I forget and get the foolish idea that the reason God gave me a wonderful wife was to keep me happy and see that I want for nothing. Sometimes I forget and get the strange thought that the reason Jesus Christ invited me to follow him was so that he could make my world more comfortable and keep me away from those nasty people who mess up my day. I forget why I am here. And so do you.

Why am I here? I am here to see that my child gets to know Jesus Christ. I am here to see that my wife meets Jesus Christ. I am here to see that my co-workers, my neighbors, my friends, my enemies and you, meet Jesus Christ. I am here to be a reflector for Jesus Christ. I am here to be number two.

And, when I honestly think about it, I can't think of a more exciting place to be.

Epiphany 3 (C, L)
Ordinary Time 3 (RC)
Matthew 4:12-23

Questions

Have you ever had news to tell someone that you were afraid to tell them because you really didn't know how they would respond? You don't want to tell them, but you know eventually you will have to? In my mind, that is how it happened.

All the way back from the well, Mary stewed. Would he be angry or sad, or say nothing at all? Would he go away, or stay here? For months he had been paying close attention to everything John had been doing. He had questioned every traveler through town for news of John, the baptizer. Mary didn't understand the deep interest, but something inside told her it would lead to no good. But she didn't know what to do about it. And she didn't know how to tell him now that John had been arrested and thrown into prison.

It began innocently enough with Herod Antipas making a trip to Rome. Why he went doesn't matter. What matters is the fact that while there he met a girl. The fact that the girl was the wife of his brother, as well as Herod's niece (the Herod family tree is a nightmare to behold), and the fact that he seduced her and ended up marrying her is what matters. Did I mention that Herod already had a wife back home he had to divorce first? Well, the whole thing broke nearly every rule relating to marriage and family relations in the Jewish law books. However, all the Jewish law teachers knew enough to keep quiet and let Mr. Herod do pretty well whatever he wanted to do, whether they approved of it or not. So no one said a word. No one except John, and he said several words.

Herod was not the kind of man to forget an enemy, and although it took him some time, and some "official" excuse, the day came when he finally had John arrested. While the official charge was the worry that John's influence was growing so great that he might lead the people to rebellion, the real charge was airing Herod's family laundry without a license.

For Herod it was a pleasure. For John, it was a nightmare. He was placed in the prison of Machaerus in the mountains east of the Dead Sea. The man who had wandered the deserts and open spaces preaching, was now thrown in a sealed dungeon cell. How would he handle that?

But Mary was more worried about how her Jesus would handle the news. She didn't have any idea of how to break it to him, but just like you and I have done, she did. From there it was his move.

I tell you all this to lead up to one sentence. There comes a time when you are finally handed the keys.

That may sound like nonsense, but it is true. There comes a time when all your preparation, all your dreaming and planning, all your waiting, comes to a crashing end, and everyone turns to you and says, "Okay, now it's your turn to drive."

The young woman has dreamed all her life of becoming a school teacher. She has been to college, taken all those education classes, like Lesson Planning 101 and "Kiddie Lit." She has spent a semester student teaching under the guidance of an older "pro," and has survived a series of interviews for her first position. Then comes that morning when they hand her the keys to the south door of the building and she walks down the hall into "her" room. She steps inside, looks around at the walls that cry for some decoration, and it hits her, "Can I do this? Can I really do this? Where do I begin? Will they like me? Will I be able to teach them anything? O Lord, what have I gotten myself into?"

The young couple walk through the front door of their little house, carrying their newborn baby daughter. They have prepared for this day. They waited until they were finished with the college degrees and most of the loans were paid. They read the books, attended childbirth classes, and rented the videos at the library on parenting. They had talked about how they would make decisions together, and how they would not push their child "like they had been pushed," and had even fully stocked the nursery all in preparation for this day. They walk in the house, close the door, and stand in the middle of the living room holding a baby in their arms. They are excited. They are also wondering if they can really pull this off. "Can we do this? Can we really do this? Where do we begin? Will she like me? Will I be able to teach her anything? What if she gets sick? Can I handle that? Oh Lord, what have we gotten ourselves into?"

He has worked 40 years for this day. Oh, it has been a good 40 years, but in the back of his mind he always had one eye on this day, when it would come to an end. He had worked hard and built a good reputation. He had made many friends. He had put back enough so that money would not be short for the two of them when the time came. He had read the books his wife had bought for him on how to deal with the new lifestyle. He was ready. But as he stood there in the cafeteria looking at the gold watch in his hand, and hearing the applause of his former co-workers, he heard himself wondering, "Can I do this? Can I really do this? Where do I begin? What if it doesn't work out like we have planned? Oh Lord, what have I gotten myself into?"

I have to wonder if, when he was handed the keys to take charge, any of this went through Jesus' mind. Matthew makes it all sound so easy. Here in 12 short verses Matthew takes Jesus from a safe second position to a preaching Messiah followed by four disciples, and makes it look painless. I really wonder about that. I'm not questioning Jesus' strength, or his ability, but I wonder, since he really was one of us, if he looked at the new keys in his hand and wondered?

It was a big decision to move from Nazareth to Capernaum. The distance between the two is geographically small, but the distance has to be measured in more than miles. In Nazareth he was home. His family was there for security. In small towns like Nazareth, no matter what else Jesus might do or say he would always be Joseph's boy from down at the carpentry shop. There was a security in that "home town advantage" even if it did cause problems for prophets. Nazareth was also fairly invisible. You could live there, and preach there, for a long time and never get quoted in the *Tiberias Times*. The town is never mentioned in the Old Testament, but it was there! Nazareth was safe.

But Capernaum! Capernaum was visible. A good-sized fishing village on the shore of the Sea of Galilee, with highways running by the edge of town and a huge synagogue right in the middle. You could preach in Capernaum and be heard all the way to Jerusalem. In Capernaum he would not be from a carpenter's shop, he would be from God. He would no longer be "Joseph's boy" but would live, and perhaps die, as God's Son. It was a long way from Nazareth to Capernaum, and I wonder if Jesus, when he heard the news about John, stood there in Nazareth looking eastward toward Capernaum, hearing himself ask "Can I do this? Can I really do this? Where do I begin? Will they follow me? Will I be able to teach them anything?"

But moving to Capernaum wasn't the only question. What would he preach once he was there? He had attended school at the synagogue and had studied the law and the prophets. He had listened to John's message and agreed that it had to be continued. He was prepared to pick up John's words and add to them what only God's own Son could add to them. But when John's voice was actually silenced in that prison cell, and Jesus was actually handed the keys, I wonder if he wondered, "Can I do this? Can I really do this? If I preach these words I will end up right where John ended up, or worse! I could temper it a bit and get a nice pulpit in a synagogue in some quiet little village and let someone else speak John's words. Oh Lord, what have I gotten myself into?"

And calling disciples. Matthew makes it sound so easy. It sounds easy for both Jesus and the new followers. But I have to wonder if it really was that easy? If Jesus called disciples, he was claiming to be someone worth following, someone worth paying attention to. It would put him, even more, in that spotlight that sometimes gets so bright it burns you. I have to wonder if when he got up that morning and walked beside the Sea of Galilee he was asking himself, "Can I do this? Can I really do this? Where do I begin? Will they really follow me? Can I really teach them anything? O Father, what have I gotten myself into?"

And I wonder if Simon, Andrew, James and John asked the same thing. Matthew makes it sound so easy for them. "At once they left their nets and followed him." They also left their families, a pretty good-sized fishing business, their home, and whatever plans they had made for their future. I have to wonder if as they followed him out of town they didn't look at each other, kind of awkwardly, and wonder inside, "Can I do this? Can I really do this? Where is this going to end up? What about the boats? What about the family? Oh Lord, what have I gotten myself into?"

I have to be honest with you and admit that I don't know if any of these men questioned any of this. Matthew never even hints that it happened. He does admit that Jesus asked a few questions later in the Garden of Gethsemane, but not now. So, for those who feel I am walking pretty near blasphemy with all these ideas, you may be right. But I hope not. I hope there were questions. I hope that the move from Nazareth to Capernaum was a difficult one. I hope that deciding what to preach was something that kept Jesus up late and woke him up early. I really hope that the decision to call disciples, and to be disciples, was frightening. Because they did it anyway. The questions could not stop them.

I find myself being stopped time and time again by the questions. Do I go here? Do I say this? Do I go along with that? Can I really teach them anything? What if they don't like me? Can I really pull this off? Where do I begin? Do I follow, or not? Oh Lord, how did I get myself into this? I hope they did ask some of these things. Because they went anyway. It would mean so much to be reminded that the questions don't really have the power to stop me.

It would mean a lot.

Epiphany 4 (C, L)
Ordinary Time 4 (RC)
Matthew 5:1-12

Ka-Chang

It was a strange sound. Some said it was a kind of "clanging" sound, while others said it was more of a "ka-ching," or more accurately, a "ka-chang!" It sounded like the result of metal hitting metal, which is exactly what it was.

In the valley off to the west from the hillside is a steep cliff rising up the face of Mount Arbel. The face of the cliff is covered with hundreds of caves, with no good way to get to them without climbing straight up the cliff. That's why the Zealots liked them. They were safe.

The Zealots were the militant group within Judaism that had declared war on Rome. Every Zealot carried a dagger under his robe and dreamed of the day when he might stick that dagger into a Roman Centurion. Zealots believed that God wanted his people free, and believing that, vowed to accept death before becoming a slave to Caesar. The Zealots found the caves of Mount Arbel to be the perfect hideout. They could swoop down during the night and carry out their terrorist raids and then climb back into the caves and be untouchable.

They slept in the caves, ate in the caves, and built their weapons in the caves. That's what everyone on the hillside was hearing. The sound of metal striking metal was the sound of the Zealot blacksmiths hammering out more daggers and swords to use against the enemy. As Jesus began to speak on the hillside, the sound of war could be heard from the valley. However, in all honesty, it seems that over here on the hillside Jesus is declaring a little war of his own.

We have heard the words of today's scripture many times. We have read them and heard them preached, and taught them in Sunday school. Usually when we have, we have heard them from the "blessed" side. We have nodded our heads when he talks to the poor in spirit, because we have been poor in spirit and appreciate the recognition. We have mourned, have felt meek, have hungered for many things including righteousness, and have tried to be merciful. We all dream of having pure hearts, like the role of peacemaker when we can get it, and certainly get our share of persecution if we put on the appearance of being too religious. The words Jesus speaks in the Beatitudes help us feel better. We know that he understands.

However, I have always wondered about the other folks. As Luke reminds us when he tells this story, the other side of "Blessed art thou," is "Woe to you" and I have always wondered how those folks felt who were on the "woe" side of the fence. I'll bet that the words they heard were a little less like "Blessed art thou" and sounded a whole lot more like "ka-chang!"

Before we begin our wondering, however, let's take a moment to meet the rest of the players. That little group on the right, standing off, kind of by themselves, are the Pharisees. They are an interesting group. They agree with a lot of what they have heard Jesus say. They believe in a resurrection from the dead, and caring for the poor, and that God can, and does, heal. However, uppermost in their minds is protecting the law. The key to all those other good things is to obey the laws of Moses, and the oral laws set forth by your rabbi. Keep your eye on the Pharisees. They have theirs on you.

That group over on the left, back in the back, dressed so nicely. Those are some Sadducees from up at Jerusalem. They have come to see that Jesus doesn't offend them, or the temple. The Sadducees couldn't care less for the poor, or the sick, or the unemployed. People get what they deserve. If they are poor, sick or unemployed, then God must want them poor, sick or unemployed, and who are we to argue with God. It is better to be rich, powerful and nicely dressed, even if that means we have to cooperate with the Romans to have those things. The Sadducees are here to see that Jesus doesn't offend the temple, or Rome. Pay them little mind. They are pretending you don't even exist.

Here and there in the crowd you see a few folks looking and sneering at the Sadducees. Those "sneerers" are some of the Zealots who have come down from Mount Arbel and are enemies with anyone who is a friend of Rome. Keep in mind, they carry daggers.

The rest of the crowd is crowd. There are some fishermen, some farmers, some tax collectors, some teachers, some prostitutes, some cancer patients, some women, some children; just good common folks. They are just hoping to hear a little hope.

This is Jesus' congregation. Now, let's try to keep score.

"Blessed are the poor in spirit." First of all, to a Sadducee, nothing "poor" is blessed. They vote no. The Zealots respect those whose spirits are strong and determined, and whose hands hold the handle of a dagger ready to act on that spirit. Zealots vote no, but do appreciate what he's trying to do for the poor. The Pharisees have no complaint. They care for the poor, and so long as they abide by the law, yes, they will be blessed. The common folk are quiet. They had never thought of themselves as blessed while their spirits were this broken. Maybe there was hope. There was a mumbled "Amen" from an old man in the cheap seats.

"Blessed are those who mourn." Most nod their heads in agreement with this one. That's probably because most of them miss the point. Jesus wasn't just talking about those who mourned the death of a family member. Who would argue with that? But what about the death of the faith? The common folks and Zealots would agree, the Pharisees, and particularly the Sadducees would not. But it probably went over their heads. This one was just a warm-up.

"Blessed are the meek." The Zealots don't like the direction this is taking. First it was "poor in spirit" and now it is "meek." This is no way to fire up a rebellion against Rome. The Pharisees and Sadducees are ticked. They have studied the old writings and know what Jesus is trying to say here. He is quoting Psalm 37 which compares the "meek" with the "wicked." The way Psalm 37 describes "wicked" comes a little too close to day-to-day behavior for Pharisees and Sadducees. This get-together has taken a nasty turn. The common folk understood, and said "Thank you."

"Blessed are those who hunger and thirst for righteousness." Everyone liked this one because they all had dreams they hungered and thirsted for. Most of them had problems catching the subtle difference between "right" and "righteousness." If they understood what he was really saying they all would have grumbled.

"Blessed are the merciful." Zealots show no mercy. They are considering going back to the cliffs. Pharisees see little room in the law for mercy. Sadducees saw no need for mercy. If God wanted people better off, he would make them better off. You got what you deserved. Many in the crowd smiled, while others, who remembered how they behave at home, ducked their heads.

"Blessed are the pure in heart." Blessed are the sincere is how it came out. They were all sincere. Again, I think they probably missed the point.

"Blessed are the peacemakers." Every eye on the hillside turned to the Zealots. It was one of those times when everyone believes the preacher has over-stepped the bounds. Sadducees wanted peace with Rome so they could stay in office. The Pharisees were for peace, within the rules of the law, which did not leave room for Rome. The Zealots were ready to kill for peace, and the common folks were thinking about how hard it was to simply be a peacemaker back home in the family.

"Blessed are you when you are persecuted for righteousness' sake." They all liked this one. They had all been persecuted at one time or another. The Sadducees felt persecuted by the ignorant poor people who didn't understand how difficult it was to be God's favored children in charge of the religious life of a nation. The Pharisees felt persecuted for their harping about all those laws. The Zealots felt persecuted by Roman Centurions carrying swords, and the common folks felt persecuted by pretty well everybody. They had all been insulted, and had evil uttered against them, and all for "righteous" reasons. But then Jesus blessed those who were laughed at for his sake. The Zealots didn't know what to do with this one. The Pharisees and Sadducees were aghast. For his sake? Blasphemy! The common folks got lost in the theology.

Let me stop here and say that the whole point of this little journey through Matthew's gospel is to show that in this lovely little collection of Beatitudes, Jesus stepped on some toes. In fact, at one point or another, he stepped on every toe in the church, I mean on the hillside. Some of them were so bruised they began to discuss how to stop him.

Sometimes the church finds itself afraid to step on toes. In fact, we find ourselves in the business of providing steel toed shoes to some folks. It's funny how Jesus almost seemed to make it a point to step on as many bare toes as he could reach in his three years.

Of course, he wasn't there to please people. He was there to save them.

Epiphany 5 (C, L)
Ordinary Time 5 (RC)
Matthew 5:13-16 (C, RC)
Matthew 5:13-20 (L)

On Being Salty

I don't remember ever meeting my Uncle Peacock. Apparently I did, but it was when I was so young that I really don't remember anything about him. But I have heard enough stories about him that I feel I know him very well. Uncle Peacock died several years ago, though all I know about his death was that it was the result of a long Saturday evening in town with a 20-pound watermelon and a chicken. It seems that somehow he ended up falling off the levee down by the river. I don't know how it all fits together, but I'm sure it makes one heck of a story.

However, I do know about the one time my Uncle Peacock fell in love. As the story goes, one summer evening he met a woman at the Rod and Gun. She was a woman from the city who wasn't too impressed with some questionable looking character who lived on the river. Did I tell you Uncle Peacock lived in a houseboat? It was a homemade kind of thing, and I guess looked as homemade as it was, but it floated well enough to give him a place to sleep when he could find his way to it. Somehow Uncle Peacock had to earn this woman's affections, and he came upon the perfect plan to do just that. Uncle Peacock decided he was going to untie his houseboat and float down the river to New Orleans. That sounded like the kind of thing to get a woman's attention, but you need to remember that this was a river town, and attention was gotten in ways there that just didn't work any place else.

So the plan was made. He stocked the boat with all the necessary supplies, most of them in liquid form, and set the date for the launching. The night before the event, all of his buddies threw Uncle Peacock a bon voyage party down at the Rod and Gun. It lasted into the wee hours of the morning. It was in one of those wee hours that Uncle Peacock decided that the time for the launch had come, and he oozed his way down to the river and his boat. It had been a long party. Uncle Peacock untied his sailing ship, pushed out into the middle of the river, and promptly fell asleep. He was on his way to New Orleans to win the hand of a lovely lady. No one is quite sure how he made it under the highway bridge, but they do know that 10 minutes later he ran smack into the upriver end of Grape Island, one mile south of town. It was there, some hours later, that Uncle Peacock woke up and realized he wasn't going to make New Orleans, and, most likely was not going to impress his girl. In his despair, he stayed there until his supplies were gone, and three weeks later swam to shore and got help. My Uncle Peacock was, my mother tells me, a "salty" kind of guy.

Much like the two old men who used to stop by our house every so often to see my dad. I was always excited when they would visit, but my mother would just groan and find something to do in another part of the house. These guys drove a big orange truck that said, "City of Beardstown" on the door, and had the job that I envied more than any other I knew. They would stand out in the middle of the intersection on our corner, and one of them would lift the cover off the manhole in the street and the other would climb right down inside of it. I never knew just what he did down there, and am still not sure I really do, but I did know that someday I wanted to do that, too!

They would work for a while and then come into our house to talk to dad and have something from the cabinet over the sink to "warm them up a bit." It may have been August, but they still needed something to help them get warm. Must have been really cold down in that hole. They would tell stories that my dad made me swear I would never tell my mother, and they laughed about things that took me another 15 years to understand well enough to chuckle at. Mom said it wasn't the stories she disliked, nor the little "warm up" from the cabinet, but the smell they brought with them. Funny, I had never noticed. Mom said that those two guys were "salty." All that I know is that when these two arrived, our house changed.

That's what salt does. It changes things. Take an ordinary, rather bland day, add a touch of salt and presto, you have something completely different. Uncle Peacock did that, and so did the men from the sewer company. The changes they brought were not always appreciated, but unavoidable for sure.

Jesus said, "You are the salt of the earth." He said that if you are going to follow him, and do things the way he wants you to, you can't help but change things wherever you go. That seems to be the blessing, and the curse, of being Christian. Things change when we arrive. I have seen it happen. I have walked into a room and have seen people actually change before my eyes. I have seen people lose one half of their entire vocabulary when I walk in. I have seen beer cans get stuffed under coffee tables and sofa pillows and other places I am sure they later regretted having stuffed them. I have seen hopeless faces in emergency rooms transform into hopeful faces when I came through the door. It's not me doing that, it's what I represent. And it's what you represent. When Christ comes in, everything changes.

Table salt in the first century was collected from the ground around the Dead Sea. Large chunks of salt-covered rock were placed on the dinner table and you simply scraped off what you needed for the meal. After a while, however, all the salt was scraped from the rock, and all you had left in the middle of your table was rock. The salt had lost its saltiness. It was good for nothing. Throw it away! Jesus said it is no different with us. What is the value of one who has lost his or her saltiness? What is the use of the Christian who leaves things tasting the way the world leaves them tasting?

Just as light changes dark into something new, and salt changes what it touches into something new, a follower of Jesus Christ changes what it touches as well. It can't be stopped. But we try, don't we? We don't actually run out of salt, but instead of spreading it around we put it on the shelf like a collection of salt shakers. Sometimes it is embarrassing to always be the one who is different. Sometimes I would like to walk into the room and just be a part of the crowd. "Don't change because of me! Just be yourself." Sometimes it is lonely to be the one who is different. Sometimes it is simply terrifying. Sometimes people who are different get killed, even crucified. No, sometimes I don't want to be the salt of the earth. But there is no choice. Christians change things simply by being there.

Jesus said that the world does things in a certain way, and measures success and failure by certain measures, but "you will not do it that way! You will change the way things are done." You cannot hide the light and you cannot stop the salt from making things salty.

Our greatest task as Christians today may well be standing close enough to each other to give each other the courage to be salty. To find the courage to be different enough to cause things to change. Because, as I look at it, we could do with a few changes.

Epiphany 6 (C, L)
Ordinary Time 6 (RC)
Matthew 5:17-26 (C)
Matthew 5:20-37 (L)
Matthew 5:17-37 (RC)

For Your Part

I walked to the bank the other day. I made my way over to one of the desks and sat down to talk to a guy whose name tag said "Andy." I said, "Andy, I need some money, and was wondering if you could help me?" Andy smiled and said he would be glad to do what he could. I told him what I needed and he left the room for a few minutes to run the credit check and whatever else it is that they do at a time like that. Minutes later he walked back in and said, "No problem, John. I've got your check right here!" He slid the money across the table. I was impressed with how easy it had been and as I started to get up Andy said, "Just a second John, I need your signature in a couple of places."

"For what?"

"Well, this one shows that you received your check, and this one shows that you understand the payment schedule."

"What payment schedule?"

"Uh, for the note. See, for our part, we give you the money, and for your part, each month you pay it back in . . ."

"Pay it back?" I interrupted. "You mean I have to pay this back? I hadn't counted on that. We'd better just forget it then." And I left.

I walked down the street to another bank I knew and sat down to talk with Howard. I explained the need I had, and the fact that I wasn't able to get the help over at the other bank. Howard said he would be glad to check it out, and moments later returned with check in hand.

"I'm not sure what the problem was down the street, John, but it looks great here. Here's your check."

Now that's more like it. I shook Howard's hand, picked up my check and turned to go.

"Wait just a second, John, I need your signature on a couple of things here."

"Signature, for what?"

"Well, this one shows that you received your check, and this one shows that you understand . . ."

"You mean the payments?"

"Right. It's just a formality to show that you understand about the interest rates and everything."

"Interest? You mean I have to pay interest, too?"

"Of course. For our part, we loan you the cash. For your part . . ."

I was out the door before I heard the rest.

Jesus sat in the middle of the crowd on the hillside. Some of them had been with him for days, even weeks, but many of them were new today. They had all come to hear his teaching. The rumors were running wild about what he was going to say. Most of the rumors were about this new kingdom he had been hinting at. Everyone was interested in a new kingdom. The one that the Romans had offered wasn't working out at all. But the age-old kingdom overseen by the priests, scribes and Pharisees had become pretty unbearable, too, what with all those laws that no one could ever hope to follow. So the rumors of a new kingdom brought them all out. Whatever he offers will be an improvement. No more old laws. No more Pharisees. That's what Jesus is going to do for us.

As far away as that day is, we can still hear the excitement in their voices as they wait to hear from him. "Shhhhhhhhhh!" He finds a rock in the middle of them, sits down, and speaks.

"Some of you are under the impression that I am going to do away with the old laws. Well, don't ever get the idea that I have come to abolish the law. In fact, not one comma or apostrophe will be changed."

The crowd was stunned.

"In fact, with me it is going to become even harder than it has been. Yessir, you see those teachers standing over there?" He pointed to a group of Pharisees watching the whole thing from a safe distance. "Do you see them? I tell you the truth, if you want in my father's kingdom, you are going to have to become even more righteous than those guys over there!"

The Pharisees smiled to each other, "More righteous than us? Who is he kidding?"

The crowds looked at the group and chuckled, "More righteous than them? We get the point. Those guys certainly know the law, no doubt about it, but righteous? No way."

The people respected the Pharisees as the keepers of the law. They kept it. They kept it tightly. They memorized it, and taught their disciples to memorize it. But follow it? That's another matter. As experts in the law, they were also experts in the loopholes.

As an example, for one of the annual holidays all Jews had to clean their homes, and throw away any foods that did not fit within the old, very rigid, dietary laws. This included any prepared foods, many spices and items the "modern" Jewish family used the rest of the year. When the holiday passed, everyone had to go to the market and repurchase items they had thrown away. It was becoming an expensive law. The Pharisees had found that with a little creative thinking it could be made cheaper. The law actually said that Jews could not own those items, or have them in their homes during the holiday. So, why not just pack the things up, take them to a non-Jewish neighbor, sell the box to them for a buck, then, buy it back after the holiday? Quick, efficient, much cheaper, and perfectly legal. If you understood the law. They were many things, yes, but righteous was not necessarily one of them.

Jesus continued, "You have heard that you shall not kill." He gazed at the teachers in the distance, and they shifted uneasily under his stare. No fewer than three previous rebel-teachers had met with crucifixion in recent years at the hands of these keepers of the law. Loopholes. These three men had come from the south teaching that God loved people more than laws. But they had been branded rebels and blasphemers, which the law said must be punished by death. Righteous? Probably not. But legal, absolutely.

The crowd, however, had its mind on the Romans. No one had made the streets flow with blood quite like the centurions had. God would certainly get them for breaking his law. "Preach it, Jesus!" someone shouted.

"You have heard that you shall not kill. But I tell you that even if you are angry with your brother, you are liable. Get angry enough to call someone "empty-head," or in other words, "air-head," or blurt out a bold "your momma!" and you are liable. Burn inside with a grudge and you will end up thrown into the fires of the Hinnon Valley, the valley at the edge of Jerusalem that burns 24 hours a day with the garbage and trash of the city, and resembles Hell itself.

"When you bring your gift to the altar, and remember that your brother has something against you, put down the gift, go fix what needs to be fixed, and then present your gift."

There. There it is. Can you imagine that? Can you picture in your mind what would happen if everyone here, before we went any further with what we are doing, got up out of their seats, went and mended all their broken relationships? Picture it. Every person in this church who has a grudge gets right up, goes to the person and gets it all settled, then sits back down. (Or every person reading this book, sticks a bookmark right here, closes the book, picks up the phone or walks out the door, gets it all worked out and settled, and then reads on?) Can you see it? That's what Jesus called for that morning on the hillside. No more hassle. No more law courts. No more!

Can you hear the people of the crowd? For some on the hillside it was too much. This is where Jesus became impossible for them. They stood, and slowly walked out of the crowd, and went back home. Many people went up that hillside to hear Jesus but could not walk back down it with him. They could be Christian on the inside, with the spiritual highs, the warm fuzzies, the deep thoughts, but not the outside. To go and forgive, or confess? To do their part? Too much. This was not the freedom they had expected.

Jesus offered a kingdom. He did his part. What remains is our part; the acting, the forgiving and the confessing. The rebuilding of broken relationships, that is our part. We have come to the hill. We have heard the "Blessed art thous" and have now been asked to sign on the line. For some of us this is where it becomes too much. Here Jesus becomes impossible for us. Inside, we have gotten up out of our seats, slowly made our way out of the crowd, and have gone home. We just won't sign for the check! Relationships remain broken, grudges continue to burn holes in our stomachs, and we wonder why Christianity just doesn't do for us what it does for others.

There is good news. The offer made on the hillside then, still stands now. The papers are still on the desk.

You can sign at any time.

Epiphany 7 (C, L)
Ordinary Time 7 (RC)
Matthew 5:27-37 (C)
Matthew 5:38-48 (L, RC)

Ooo Boy!

I don't know what started the argument. I don't know if anyone really knows what started the argument. In all honesty, it doesn't matter. I think we all know that most arguments never end up where they end up because of where they started. It might have started over some disagreement over the children. It might have begun over something about the in-laws, or perhaps it was her cooking again. Who knows. But it really doesn't matter how it started, what matters is that it has suddenly gotten very quiet in the room.

They sit staring at each other across the table with a look in their eyes that frightens them both. He takes a deep breath, pushes himself back from the table, stands and walks out the door. Not a word is spoken. Minutes later he comes back in the door, this time with two of his friends. He walks over, sits down at the table, takes a piece of paper and a pencil from his pocket and begins to write. When he is finished, he puts the pencil back in his pocket and slides the note across the table to his wife. She opens it and reads, "I, Reuben, divorce you, Elizabeth." Their eyes meet again, just for a second, and he stands. And it is done. It is over. It is legal. They are divorced.

According to the old law, as we can still read in the Mishnah, a man can divorce his wife simply by writing the words of divorce on a piece of paper and handing it to his wife in the presence of two witnesses. And it is done.

Oh, it is sad. It ended for them so differently than it had begun. It is sad because the Jewish people of the first century had such a high regard for marriage. Marriage between man and woman was something that was in God's hands. It was sacred, holy and good.

What has happened? How has it come to a point where all a man need do is scribble words on paper and it is done? If marriage is so sacred, what has happened?

Rome has happened. But in all honesty, I can't blame it all on Rome because the Roman Empire began with a vision of marriage almost higher than that of the Jewish nation. To the Romans, in the beginning, marriage was so sacred that for the first 500 years of the empire, there was not one recorded divorce. Five hundred years, no divorce. But then something began to change.

What happened was the Greeks. The Roman Empire militarily defeated the Greek Empire. The richness of the old Greek culture began to assimilate into the young Roman Empire. The Greeks were defeated militarily, but not morally. It was the Greek viewpoint toward marriage that began to bring change.

To the Greeks there were three kinds of women. There were the courtesans, the concubines and the wives. Top of the line were the courtesans. They were the most highly respected of women. They were the finest dressed, finest educated, the finest companion for a man. These were the women you would take with you to a business convention and wanted to make a good impression. Take your beautiful courtesan with you and enjoy her beauty, wit and intelligence. She was there to make you happy and successful. But she was not your wife.

Secondly was the concubine. She was there to live with. She was for pleasure at home and to bring you a smile after a long, difficult day. She was entertainment. She did not carry the status of the courtesan, yet was an important woman in her man's life. But she was not your wife.

Finally, ranking somewhere below the other two, was the wife. The wife was the most highly protected and treasured of the three. She was so highly protected and treasured that she was rarely ever allowed to leave the home and risk contamination by the outside world. She stayed at home in her role of caring for the household. She raised the children. She kept things together. She was the center of it all, but the center of it all is not always a good place to be.

It was not only accepted, but expected, that in addition to a wife, the Greek husband would have the concubines and the courtesan. It was expected that the Greek husband would be unfaithful to his wife. But it wasn't really unfaithfulness, it was "just the way things were done."

The Greeks had the ideal of marriage that every husband would be loyal to one wife. That was the ideal, the way it should be done. But they all knew it just wasn't reality. That was just not the way it was being done, and even if it was the way it ought to be, sometimes reality isn't ideal. Could we really expect people to change to fit some dream? There were years and years of tradition behind this. Rome defeated the Greeks militarily, but not morally. The longer the Greek Empire touched the Roman Empire, the more the morals of the Greeks became the morals of the Romans. And as Rome spread its authority over the Israelites, the more the morals of the Romans became the morals of the Jews. The Jews had their ideals of marriage. They remembered the old laws. The rabbis still taught the old laws to their disciples, who would teach them to theirs. They all knew the ideal "One husband has one wife, for life." They believed in the ideal. But, they also knew that ideals are seldom really attained.

So within this very loyal Jewish theology, two schools began to develop. The followers of Rabbi Shammai believed that the ideal was worth fighting for, and that the only possible ground for divorce was unfaithfulness. If husband or wife was ever unfaithful to the other, then the other partner was free to divorce. That was the only ground. This group was respected for their idealistic views, but laughed at as unrealistic and old fashioned.

The second school, that of Rabbi Hillel, focused on a passage from Deuteronomy 24 which says that a man shall divorce his wife on the grounds of unchastity, or "if she finds no favor in his eyes." It is a small line in chapter 24, but it was not little to Rabbi Hillel. From there it is pure interpretation. Divorce is acceptable in the case of unfaithfulness, or if the wife happened to put a bit too much salt in the evening meal. A woman using too much salt may not find favor in the eyes of her husband. Or perhaps, one afternoon during his walk through the marketplace, the husband sees an attractive young woman standing over by the oranges and tangerines. As he looks at her, he pictures in his mind his wife of 23 years who has given him seven children, and looks nothing like the young thing before him. In his mind, his wife no longer holds the favor that this new vision holds. So, those are grounds for divorce. Oh, there were the old laws. But there were also loopholes. There were always loopholes.

Marriage became something different. It became something difficult, something uncertain. If the only way to end a marriage was unfaithfulness then you could remain faithful and feel fairly secure in your marriage, but if your marriage revolved around whether the husband happened to see some attractive, new young thing down the road, where is the security? Marriage became so uncertain that many young girls of the first century chose not to get married, rather than risk the uncertain future. It was believed that marriage was almost doomed to fail. "Most marriages fail, so why even begin?" The very tradition of family began to shake at its foundations. And it was more than that. Where do we teach the old stories of the faith? At the family table. Where do they hear of Abraham and Isaac? At the family table. The foundations of the family, and of the kingdom itself, were being threatened with destruction.

Into that Jesus walks to the side of a hill one sunny morning. As he talks and explains his beliefs and understandings, he says, "You have heard it said that whoever divorces his wife let him give her a certificate of divorce and it is done.

But I say to you, that whoever, anyone, who divorces his wife, except on the grounds of unchastity, makes her an adultress."

Ooo boy! Now, the question. Is he serious? This is difficult preaching here. There are people in every congregation that this touches. Is he really saying what I think he's saying? We might be better off to just skip this passage, and many times we have done just that. Other times we have used this passage as a club to pound people over the head with guilt. Most of the time we simply shake our heads and walk away, confused.

But I believe there is an answer. To find it you have to listen a little longer to what Jesus says. He doesn't stop talking and sit down after he talks about marriage. He goes on to say, "And the same goes for all those other oaths and promises you make. You make vows in the name of Jerusalem, or in the name of Israel, or in the name of Abraham. No more! Don't swear by these." Everyone knew very well that any vow made in one of these names could be broken. They were promises that were kept unless something else, more favorable, came up. He said, "Forget all this breaking of vows and promises, whether it is in business, or in marriage. Let your 'Yes' be 'Yes,' and your 'No' be 'No.' In my Father's kingdom anything else is simply unacceptable."

The issue here is not only marriage, but your "word." In a marriage relationship, or in business, or in living day-to-day with the people around you, your "word" must stand. Relationships will be broken and end, that is reality. But the follower of Jesus Christ will not be the cause.

Difficult words!

But I say to you, that whoever, anyone, who divorces his wife, except on the grounds of unchastity, makes her an adulteress.

Epiphany 8 (C, L)
Ordinary Time 8 (RC)
Matthew 5:38-48 (C)
Matthew 6:24-34 (L, RC)

Les

I like the first part of this story about Jesus. All those blessings, and that neat parable about the salt of the earth, and the light of the world. It makes me feel good inside. But now it gets difficult. Let me put this in terms that I can understand.

The first time I ever remember hating anyone was in the third grade. The kid's name was Les. Les moved into town part way through the year and from the beginning we had trouble. On the first day, I received a note during spelling. The note read, "After school. You're dead!" The note was signed, "Les." This was not good news, as Les stood about six-foot tall and weighed in the area of 200 pounds. In the third grade! Fortunately, I had to stay a few minutes late after school that afternoon, and by the time I left, so had everyone else. I found several new paths home and managed to avoid Les for over a week. Until the inevitable happened. I forgot.

I walked out of school one afternoon and crossed the street towards home, when out from behind a bush stepped Les. A huge crowd suddenly showed up. They all apparently knew what was going to happen and didn't want to miss it. Les took one step toward me and I took one step back. I negotiated. I asked why this was happening. Neither God nor Les would give me a reason. Les took another step toward me and I took another step back. I looked at the audience and smiled a smile that was supposed to say "I'm not worried," you know, to look cool. But the look in my eyes apparently blew the image and everyone laughed. Big old Les took another step toward me and I took another step back. And I tripped over the fire hydrant and fell backwards, rolling down the ditch next to the road, and landed in the mud. It was hilarious. At least that's what they all thought. Les hadn't laid a hand on me but had destroyed every ounce of pride, self-esteem and dignity in my body. Everybody laughed and went home, by way of Les' house where they all got ice cream first. Oh, how I hated that kid. She was the meanest woman I have ever met in my life!

I sat there in the mud thinking that life couldn't be any worse. I was wrong. Two weeks later, while my mother and I were planning my upcoming birthday party, she said, "Why don't you invite the new girl in your class to your party?" I gave every reason I could think of not to invite her, I even told the truth! But in the end I had to invite her. That's what I was told. So I did the only thing an honest, healthy third grader could do. I lied. I never invited Les to the party. I told Mom that Les was going out of town and couldn't come. It was a week after the party, which, by the way was one of the grandest events ever held in Beardstown with the entire third grade class of Beard School attending (except for one), when I went with Mom to the store. We were walking down the cereal aisle when we met Les' mother. My mother said, "I'm so sorry Les missed the party." I prayed. Les' mom answered, "What party?" I prayed real hard. It didn't help.

I will spare you the details of our ride home, and the next few weeks of confinement, but just let me say that I have never hated anyone quite like I hated that third grade girl. I still occasionally have dreams of getting even.

The sermon was going strong. Everyone had found a soft spot to sit, and had gotten the children settled down enough to pay attention to what Jesus was saying. Except for this one guy who came wandering in late. He had missed all the "Blessed are thous," and was obviously not in a good mood.

He made so much racket finding a place to sit that Jesus finally stopped preaching, looked over at the guy, and asked, "Do you have a problem?" The guy almost exploded. He apologized for being late and disturbing everyone, but said he had just about had it up to here! It seems that on his way to the hillside he had been stopped by a Roman soldier. The soldier was traveling through the area and said that he wanted the guy to carry this big suitcase a mile down the road. To make it worse, after they had gone the mile, the soldier said that he really liked the guy's new coat, and wanted it for himself. The coat had been a gift from the man's wife, but now it was in the hands of some red-necked centurion who wouldn't appreciate fine weaving if it jumped out and bit him! This guy was furious.

And as he talked, the crowd became furious, too. It had happened to most all of them at one time or another. They all knew the laws. If a Roman stopped you and asked you to carry their bag a mile, you had to do it. You had no choice. They were Roman, you were not. And if a Roman stopped you and asked for your coat, you had to give it to them. Same rule. They were Roman, you were not. Jesus sat there and listened to one story after another as the crowd joined in what was fast becoming a top of the line gripe session. Finally, he jumped in and said "I'll tell you what. The next time some soldier stops you and asks you to carry their bag one mile, carry it two miles!" He had their attention. "And the next time one of them wants you to give them your coat, give it to them. Then take off your shirt and hand that to them, too. It will drive them nuts!" While they were still in shock, he kept talking, and in all honesty, this is where Jesus loses me.

He said "Love your enemies." He spent some time expanding on that idea, explaining that we should turn the other cheek instead of swinging back, and that we should give to others who take advantage of us and have no intention of giving back. He says that it is well and good to like those people who like you, and do things the way you want them done, but the real test of what you're made of is if you can like those people who just aren't likable, who do everything possible to push you away. Later on he even suggests that when we have parties it is more important to invite our enemies than our friends. I'm sure he wasn't talking about birthday parties. I am quite sure that someone like Les has to be the exception.

Hey, if you get your exceptions, I get mine! We all make them, don't we? We all remember Jesus' words about enemies, but we also know that there are some enemies that fall outside the rules. We all know full well that there are some enemies who really need to be ignored. We all know full well that there are some enemies who need to be put down, insulted and talked about over coffee down at the restaurant. We all know very well that there are some enemies who are so hopeless, we have no choice but to go to war with them. So we put out our arsenal of words, stares, stealth bombers and laser-guided smart bombs and do what we know must be done. There are exceptions aren't there.

It has been painful to watch my daughter learn about the exceptions. She has heard me talk at home and preach at church about forgiving our enemies, and turning the other cheek, only to ask me about that when I make some comment about that obnoxious old woman who keeps telling everyone that my preaching is a waste of time. My daughter asks me about that "forgive our enemies" talk, and I try to explain to her about "exceptions" but she hasn't seemed to catch on. Until now. She is now in the sixth grade and is beginning to understand. Now I see her making the exceptions that I have made. She understands what Jesus said, she has heard it in Sunday school and at home. But she now also understands that there are exceptions. I am sorry to see that.

The crowd on the hillside was as confused as I am. Can he be saying what it sounds like he is saying? Sure, the law says we have to tolerate these enemies, but love them? I mean, he is suggesting we get careless here. To turn the other cheek to an enemy gives a pretty good chance we are going to get whopped on it. That would be a second time, and that would be foolish. If we give to anyone who asks, and loan without expecting to get anything in return, doesn't that put us in a rather awkward position? Doesn't he realize that is going to make us look like a bunch of clowns? We are going to get pushed over fire hydrants, and stripped of our coats, and we are going to spend the better part of some days carrying someone else's suitcases who knows where! What will people think?

There must be exceptions here. Can Jesus really be asking us to love all our enemies, even big old Leslie? Does he really expect us to do that?

Yep.

Transfiguration (C, L)
Matthew 17:1-9

Coming Back Down

I have visited some places I really wish I could have stayed. If it were my choice I would still be there right now. As much as I like it here, I would rather be there.

There is a tent, set on a hill at the top of a 1,500-foot cliff overlooking the Jordan Valley in southern Israel. When the sun comes up in the morning it breaks over the mountains a few miles to the east and literally shatters the darkness around you. The winds sail up the face of the cliff from the valley below and almost make you believe you could lean out into them and fly away. It is quiet. No phone. No traffic. It is the area that Moses wandered for 40 years. I could do that. I could stay there.

There was a day that I sat in the little green room at Decatur Memorial Hospital. I had just become a father. I sat in a chair holding this little blanket in my arms. Inside the blanket were two blue eyes. The eyes looked straight into mine and said things that I could not hear, but could feel more clearly than I had felt anything in my life. My daughter. MY daughter. I would like to go back there. I would like to spend some time there again, seeing those eyes. Oh, the eyes are still here, but now they are 12 years old and look at many different things. Then, they looked at me. Only me. I am proud of my

12-year-old, but, I could go back to that room again. I could stay there.

Or at the end of the aisle at the little church in Beardstown. Someone was singing some song and I stood there looking at my bride. We hadn't said "I do" yet, and I wasn't sure I was even capable of those words. But, there she stood. Her eyes were still red from the tears of excitement. My palms were so sweaty I wiped them on my rented pants. She looked at me and smiled. It was so innocent. She had no idea what she was getting into. Her trust was overwhelming. She moved something down deep inside me that had never before budged. I wish I could go back there again. Oh, my bride is still here, some 20 years later, but now she knows. She knows about the temper, the pouting, the laziness, the childishness. She means more to me now than I thought anyone could ever mean to me, but I could still go back. I could go stand at that altar forever, looking into her trust and feeling like she made me feel. As nice as it is here, I could go back in a minute.

I think Peter would understand that. I think that whatever else happened in Peter's life, and we have an awful lot of it recorded, he would have given it all up to go back. And I think I know where he would have gone.

It was a mountain. Nobody agrees today which mountain it was, although there are two top contenders for the title. It was Jesus, James, John and Peter who went up. I will leave it to the theologians to explain what happened up there and will just tell you the way Matthew tells it to me. The four of them walked up the mountain. Just days before, Jesus had told his disciples that story about "picking up your cross" and had assured them that some of them would have to make that choice, so I am sure there was some discussion taking place on the way up. When they reached the top it happened. While they stood there together, Jesus' face began to change. He began to glow, or shine like the light of the sun. His clothing lit up like a detergent commercial. Then, suddenly, there were two more standing with them. There stood Moses, and next to him, Elijah. Peter was overwhelmed. He made his decision right then and there. He blurted out to Jesus, "Lord, this is wonderful. How about if I build us some shelter up here and we just stay?" But before he could finish his sentence God interrupted and drove Peter, James and John to their knees. God has that kind of voice sometimes. When they looked back up, it was over. Jesus had started toward the trail back down the mountain. But I think Peter would like to have stayed.

It happens that way. Some here this morning have had that kind of experience. That time in your life when suddenly you knew who Jesus was, and found that everything in the world looked different now that you recognized him. Suddenly everything made sense, and the things that didn't make sense didn't matter. And you really wished you could stay right there. "Let's not go back down the mountain where all those people are wanting all that stuff. Let's stay up here and visit with Moses and Elijah, and hear a bit more from God." Some of us have had the mountaintop experience, and have not wanted to come back down.

Coming back down from the mountain is hard. Most people don't understand what happened up there, and the more you try to explain it, the more they smile that smile at you. Some people do understand, because they have been up there before, too, but it was a long time ago, and they have forgotten what it was like, or, more frightening, have decided that the trip really hadn't made any difference. We don't want to become like them.

It is hard down here. There are noises here that don't exist on the mountaintop. We are asked to do things here that no one up there asks us to do. We have to make decisions down here that just never come up on the mountaintop. So, some of us decide to go back to the mountain, and stay. It is much easier. On the mountaintop we can enjoy the rush of the experience and the view, without being bothered by what goes on down below. We aren't troubled by the valley's decisions and temptations. The mountaintop is the place to be.

Marriage changes. Everyday we try to look at each other with that same rosy-colored glaze on our eyes that was there that day we stood together on the mountaintop. That gaze filters out so much of what has happened between us and pretends it never happened. But things have happened. We are different people than we were that day. But that is not a bad thing. Living together in the valley means getting to know more and more of each other. Sure, some things are difficult and unpleasant, but many are wonderful surprises, and marvelous gifts. A marriage of 20 years has the chance to be so much deeper and stronger than one of a few days, if we are willing to watch it grow. If we strive to protect it, and keep it away from change, not only do we miss the opportunity to grow closer together in love, but we run the risk of growing further apart by not recognizing how we both have changed. You can't stay on the mountain.

I find myself, at times, trying to run back into that room at the hospital. Twelve-year-olds ask questions that never came up back there. Sometimes I find myself looking at my daughter and not seeing any of her. What I see is that bundle with the two blue eyes that never argued, never challenged, never disobeyed. But the more I try to stay there, the more I miss. We lose so much when we refuse to allow our children to grow up. It is difficult to do, and painful to endure, but it must be allowed to happen. A 12-year-old must be cared for differently than an infant. Freedoms are demanded. Discipline is required. If I look at her as something less than who she is, we both lose. As much as I enjoyed the blue eyes staring innocently into my own, I must let her grow. Her blue eyes are pretty amazing at age 12. You cannot stay on the mountain.

We have climbed the mountain with Peter, and have followed him, sometimes unwillingly, back down. We have had those moments of awe, when we have fallen to our knees and said "Wow!" and we have had those moments of terror and frustration when we have cried out "enough!" They go together. There is no reason to fear coming back down. When the questions arise in your faith, it may be growth instead of death. When the questions arise in your marriage, it may be growth instead of death. When the questions arise in your parenting, it may be growth and not death.

Peter would not have become who he was if he hadn't gone up that mountain with Moses, Elijah and Jesus.

We wouldn't be who we are — if he hadn't come back down.

www.ingramcontent.com/pod-product-compliance
Lightning Source LLC
Chambersburg PA
CBHW060848050426
42453CB00008B/899